Crime Prevention and Security Management

Series Editor
Martin Gill
Perpetuity Research
Tunbridge Wells, UK

It is widely recognized that we live in an increasingly unsafe society, but the study of security and crime prevention has lagged behind in its importance on the political agenda and has not matched the level of public concern. This exciting new series aims to address these issues looking at topics such as crime control, policing, security, theft, workplace violence and crime, fear of crime, civil disorder, white collar crime and anti-social behaviour. International in perspective, providing critically and theoretically-informed work, and edited by a leading scholar in the field, this series will advance new understandings of crime prevention and security management.

More information about this series at
http://www.palgrave.com/gp/series/14928

Morgan Burcher

Social Network Analysis and Law Enforcement

Applications for Intelligence Analysis

Morgan Burcher
Faculty of Arts and Education
Deakin University
Victoria, VIC, Australia

Crime Prevention and Security Management
ISBN 978-3-030-47770-7   ISBN 978-3-030-47771-4   (eBook)
https://doi.org/10.1007/978-3-030-47771-4

This Palgrave Macmillan imprint is published by the registered company Springer Nature Switzerland AG
The registered company address is: Gewerbestrasse 11, 6330 Cham, Switzerland

Foreword

By way of introduction, my name is Associate Professor David Bright. I lead the Flinders Illicit Networks Lab at Flinders University in Adelaide, Australia. My lab is one of only few labs internationally dedicated to the study of illicit networks. I am also Deputy Director of the Centre for Crime Police and Research, one of the foremost centres for criminological research internationally.

I have been conducting research on illicit networks, mostly organised criminal groups and terrorist groups, over more than a decade. Much of my research, and the research undertaken in the Flinders Illicit Networks Lab, employs social network analysis (SNA) to examine the social structure and dynamics of such illicit networks. As a forensic psychologist and criminologist, I'm intrigued by both sociological and psychological explanations for individual and group-based criminal behaviour and the complementarities across these two sets of explanatory mechanisms. I remember my first introduction to networks and SNA, an introductory book on the subject, and being struck by the potential that a network perspective offered to elucidate the macro social structure of illicit groups, the nature of smaller subgroups or cliques and the contribution and influence of individuals within such groups. Much of my own work has focused on the utility of social network analysis to identify the strengths and vulnerabilities of illicit networks and to understand how law enforcement agencies can capitalise on these network vulnerabilities to generate effective crime prevention and intervention strategies.

The community of criminal networks researchers internationally is relatively small, but growing. I have been lucky enough to work with some of the most amazing and talented scholars in this space across the globe. My journey through the illicit networks field led me to collaborate with international experts in the field, and among them a small group of talented researchers here in Australia including the author of this book, Dr Morgan Burcher (when he was a PhD student), and his supervisor Associate Professor Chad Whelan from Deakin University.

Given the focus of my research, I have been consistently interested in the extent to which law enforcement, intelligence and security agencies use SNA, how they use it, how effectively they employ such analyses and what challenges they face in employing such techniques. The answers to these questions have remained elusive for me and for other criminal networks researchers. And this brings me to the important and unique contribution this book makes to the literature on illicit networks. Dr Burcher is one of very few researchers to address this important gap in the academic literature on criminal networks: the use of SNA by law enforcement agencies in intelligence collection and operational policing. This is no easy undertaking, and may explain why few have managed to conduct such research. Gaining relevant ethics approvals, support from law enforcement agencies and the trust of sometimes highly suspicious and guarded (often for very good reason!) intelligence and security agents is a significant achievement. This book is the unique output of that achievement.

The key areas covered in the book will be of interest to students of criminology and policing, academics who study illicit networks and, of course, those at the coal face who conduct intelligence collection and investigation, including those tasked with managing intelligence analysts. The key topics of the book include: (1) the application of SNA as an investigative tool for criminal intelligence; (2) whether and how SNA is being used operationally by intelligence analysts; (3) the characteristics of criminal networks and how such characteristics create challenges in the use of SNA in operational environments and (4) the peculiar challenges of organisational environments and the implications for SNA including the focus of investigators, working relationships (especially between operational police and management) and the unique challenges that arise in the use of information technology platforms and SNA software.

This book makes a significant and very unique contribution to the literature on illicit networks more broadly, and specifically on the use of SNA by law enforcement, security and intelligence agencies. Researchers who use SNA to study various aspects of organised criminal groups and terrorist groups are interested in how SNA is used in operational contexts, how such use could be improved and how the challenges associated with using SNA in such contexts can be addressed. This book provides researchers with some answers to these questions. Researchers are also very keen to know how their research can be used to improve practice and policy in the field. On the other hand, intelligence analysts often desire to read the work of researchers to get a sense of how to extend their understanding and use of SNA. This book will appeal to both researchers and practitioners, and may even help to bridge the gap between the two groups by stimulating possibilities for collaborative work across the divide.

Adelaide, SA, Australia   David Bright

Acknowledgements

There are a number of people I must thank, for without their support this book would not have been possible. I must start by thanking Victoria Police and New South Wales Police Force for providing access to their staff. In particular, I must thank the 27 intelligence analysts that generously gave up their time to participate in this study. While I am unable to name them, there were several members of each organisation that also took the time to answer any further questions I had for which I am immensely grateful.

I would also like to sincerely thank my colleagues at Deakin University: Associate Professor Darren Palmer, Dr Wendy O'Brien, Dr Ian Warren, Dr Richard Evans and Dr Emma Ryan. In particular, I would like to thank Associate Professor Chad Whelan for his guidance, support and friendship over many years.

Finally, I must thank my friends and family for their support over many years leading up to this point. In particular, I must thank my parents, Richard and Gail, and my parents-in-law, Bill and Wilma, for your immense support and encouragement. To my partner, Casey, I will forever be grateful for your love and support over what has been a long journey. This book would not have been possible without you.

Contents

Abbreviations

ACIC	Australian Criminal Intelligence Commission
AFP	Australian Federal Police
CCR	Call charge records
CIU	Crime Investigation Unit
DIU	Divisional Intelligence Unit
DNA	Dynamic Network Analysis
ILP	Intelligence-led policing
IM	Instant messaging
IT	Information technology
OMCG	Outlaw motorcycle gang
SNA	Social network analysis
TIO	Tactical Intelligence Officer
UK	United Kingdom
US	United States
VoIP	Voice over internet protocol

Series Editor's Introduction

Social network analysis (SNA) is described as 'an analytical tool that examines the social relationships that exist within social entities' and in this book it is applied to the much neglected research area of criminal networks. Its importance for policing is that SNA affords the opportunity to better understand how gangs or organised groups are structured and the nature of information flows between members.

To-date research has focused on a retrospective analysis, rather than focusing on current operations. This book redresses this and is based on interviews with intelligence analysts in two Australian state law enforcement agencies. It looks at how SNA is used in practice and the challenges analysts then face. Specific techniques are discussed. For example, you will learn about the 3-I model, depicted as a triangle, each side representing one of three elements: *interpreting* the criminal environment, *influencing* decision-makers and having an *impact* on the crime. Read on to learn about 'boundary-specification rules' and their appropriateness for use by intelligence analysts, the value of an 'active library' and the challenge of keeping it up to date.

Indeed, there are a variety of challenges that are covered in this book. Software is one, for although it has improved markedly, developments have not kept pace with the amount of data now being collected and stored by law enforcement. Moreover, analysts are expected to be competent in a large number of software programs in order to fulfil their role but this limits their capacity to become highly knowledgeable in one or two analytical approaches, such as SNA, and the associated software.

Then there are difficulties with the data, which are often inaccurate. There are limits on the size of the networks analysts can examine. Indeed, while analysts felt that SNA was best used on large networks, they predominantly focused on small groups and increasingly smaller ones. And while SNA is best utilised in proactive investigations where it can be used to identify further avenues of inquiry, this rarely happened to its full potential with a bigger focus on the more traditional area of reactive investigations.

Personnel are also a barrier and therefore an opportunity. The majority of analysts reported both positive and negative working relationships with detectives. The single biggest factor influencing the relationship between analysts and detectives was the level of knowledge a detective had about intelligence; sadly, this was often lacking. This was less the case with senior managers who largely recognised the value of intelligence albeit were generally less informed on the mechanics of how it worked. Given that detectives and managers have considerable influence over the type of work undertaken by analysts and the actions taken as a result of their intelligence reports this, Morgan Burcher notes, educating them is a key opportunity for change. Training was also an issue for analysts. They reported that the training they received was at times inadequate and complicated by the requirement of some to undertake other duties. The author highlights the benefits of specialisation: becoming subject matter experts on a small number of analytical techniques.

In short, the author finds value in SNA as an investigative tool, including its ability to identify key actors and further avenues of enquiry: identifying information gaps and persons of interest that were previously unknown to detectives. The task then is to act on the findings of this book which is a must read for anyone working or interested in improving criminal investigation generally or tackling organised crime specifically.

March 2020

Martin Gill

1

Introduction: Intelligence-Led Policing, Crime Intelligence and Social Network Analysis

Introduction

The past two decades have seen considerable change occur within law enforcement and crime intelligence agencies. For example, along with the rest of society, law enforcement agencies have entered what is commonly referred to as the 'information age' (Arquilla 2014; Castells 2004; Medina 2014). The outcome has been a dramatic increase in the amount of information both produced and recorded by law enforcement agencies, creating numerous challenges as to how these data are collected, collated and analysed (Arquilla 2014; Brodeur and Dupont 2006; Hauck et al. 2002). A further change has been the blurring of the lines between the domains of law enforcement and national security following many high-profile terrorist attacks, including the 11 September 2001 hijackings and the 7 July 2005 London bombings (Brodeur and Dupont 2006; Coyne and Bell 2011b; Stainer 2013). There have also been changes in the criminal environment with the emergence of 'new' crime problems, including cybercrime and cyber terrorism (Taylor et al. 2014). These changes have forced law enforcement agencies to find new ways of understanding and responding to crime. Many law enforcement agencies have turned to

© The Author(s) 2020   **1**
M. Burcher, *Social Network Analysis and Law Enforcement*, Crime Prevention and
Security Management, https://doi.org/10.1007/978-3-030-47771-4_1

technology to complement longstanding policing and criminal intelligence practices (Taylor et al. 2007). For example, while law enforcement has a long history of attempting to map criminal networks (Harper and Harris 1975), due to access to powerful computing this can now be undertaken far more easily and on a scale that was largely not possible in the past. At the forefront of this more advanced form of criminal network mapping is social network analysis (SNA), a methodology that has received considerable attention as it has the potential to be of significant value to law enforcement agencies contending with a changing policing landscape.

SNA is an analytical tool that examines the social relationships that exist within social entities (Borgatti et al. 2013) such as a criminal network. It is reportedly capable of identifying the overall structure of a network (such as sub-groups), how information flows between members of a network, important individuals and possible targets for disruption (Bright et al. 2012). Reported capabilities such as these have contributed to a great deal of interest in the application of SNA to criminal networks and what it may offer law enforcement as an investigative tool. For example, Borgatti et al. (2009, p. 892) noted that network-related research is a popular topic, with 'the number of articles in the Web of Science on the topic of "social networks" nearly tripling in the past decade'. Within the field of criminology specifically, 'to find a manuscript using SNA methods is no longer rare, as both mainstream and specialty journals are now regularly publishing papers using network methods' (Bouchard and Amirault 2013, p. 119). There is now a large body of literature that has advanced our understanding of criminal networks by providing insight into the structural properties and *modus operandi* of such groups (Ball 2016; Bright et al. 2015a; Koschade 2006; Morselli 2014). Despite the intense interest in SNA, the research to date has been largely confined to retrospective analyses of past criminal networks, often years after they were in operation (Bouchard and Nash 2015). This is understandable given the well-documented difficulty in gaining access to law enforcement data due to security concerns (Bright et al. 2012; Klerks 1999; Krebs 2002; Sparrow 1991). However, this means we know almost nothing about the use of SNA within operational law enforcement environments, and this constitutes a critical gap in our understanding of the capabilities and limitations of SNA. As Mullins (2012a, p. 19) noted, if we are 'to take SNA to the next level as an investigative tool, there is a clear need for improved understanding about how it is already being used' within operational law enforcement environments.

This book provides an in-depth examination of SNA within operational law enforcement environments. It draws on the existing SNA and intelligence literature, as well as qualitative interviews with intelligence analysts from two Australian state law enforcement agencies, to examine whether and how practitioners can utilise the reported capabilities of SNA. The views of intelligence analysts offer unique insights into the role of this analytical methodology within law enforcement. The book provides an original contribution to both intelligence and SNA literature. It is the first study to explore the use of SNA by law enforcement in Australia and, more broadly, the first study to examine the use of SNA from the perspective of intelligence analysts. The primary objectives of this book are twofold: (1) to identify whether SNA is being used by intelligence analysts in operational law enforcement environments in Australia, and if so how; and (2) to determine what challenges intelligence analysts face when applying network analysis concepts and techniques to criminal networks.

This introductory chapter provides the context for this study and defines several key terms, including 'intelligence-led policing', 'crime intelligence', 'network analysis' and 'social network analysis'. It is important that terms such as network and network analysis are clearly defined, as such concepts are often used in different ways (Whelan 2012). The inconsistent use of such concepts has led to confusion within the intelligence and security fields (Whelan and Dupont 2017). The first section briefly examines some of the historical conceptual frameworks of law enforcement to better understand the latest iteration, intelligence-led policing (ILP). As ILP has been widely adopted by law enforcement agencies both in Australia and abroad (Carter and Carter 2009; Ratcliffe 2016), it is useful to understand the contextual environment in which SNA might be used. This is because the policing model adopted by law enforcement agencies heavily dictates how intelligence is used, including analytical tools like SNA. To achieve this the chapter examines the '3-I model', a framework of how ILP is intended to work within law enforcement agencies, with 'crime intelligence' at its core. Attention then turns to an overview of SNA, including an outline of what differentiates it from other forms of analysis and existing claims about what it can offer law enforcement. This chapter then presents the research design of this study, explaining why semi-structured interviews provided the best opportunity for developing new insight into the use of SNA within operational law enforcement environments. The chapter concludes with a brief outline of the book's structure.

Conceptual Frameworks of Law Enforcement

A number of policing paradigms developed during the second half of the twentieth century. These include: community-oriented policing (or simply community policing), problem-oriented policing and CompStat (computer statistics or comparative statistics). It is important to examine these frameworks as they have influenced the development of ILP, which is both the latest iteration in policing (Ratcliffe 2016), and a focal topic for this study. While each of these policing frameworks has similarities, there are differences in their philosophy and the tactics they employ (Ratcliffe 2016). Community-oriented policing places a heavy focus on 'community involvement in crime prevention efforts' (Gill et al. 2014, p. 402). While there is no agreed-upon definition of community-oriented policing (McGarrell et al. 2007; Ratcliffe 2016), Taylor (2006) observed that among the different definitions there are several common themes, including a focus on providing greater autonomy to front-line officers to foster relationships with the community. Community-oriented policing is a heavily studied topic, with much of the focus on assessing its effectiveness (Fruhling 2007; Gill et al. 2014; Liederbach et al. 2008; Van Brunsuhot 2003). For example, a systematic review of 25 studies containing 65 independent tests of community-oriented policing, with the majority conducted in the United States (US), found that while community-oriented policing improved citizen satisfaction, perceptions of disorder and police legitimacy, community-oriented policing had limited impact on reducing incidents of crime and the fear of crime (Gill et al. 2014). This may in part help to explain why many law enforcement agencies looked to move on to other policing frameworks in an effort to more effectively reduce crime, while maintaining some community policing programmes that are popular with citizens (Skogan 2006). Emerging out of the US, problem-oriented policing, developed by Herman Goldstein (1979, p. 257), 'calls for the police to take greater initiative in attempting to deal with problems rather than resign themselves to living with them'. It involves analysing a wide range of information sources (including criminal databases, informants and the community) for reoccurring problems in order to develop response strategies (McGarrell et al. 2007). This focus on the community bears clear similarities to community-oriented policing (the two are sometimes bracketed together). However, problem-oriented policing is generally regarded as having a much greater emphasis on analysing available information and trying to target the underlying causes of crime (Ratcliffe 2016). It is claimed that it allows for a shift away from the reactive style of law enforcement that has dominated since the inception of professional policing in favour of a problem-solving orientation (Rogers 2010). It has been suggested that while problem-oriented policing is easy to define, it is difficult to adopt, requiring a significant investment in analytical resources, a willingness to allow policing priorities to be grounded in analysis, and for evidence to be the key determinant in designing responses (Ratcliffe 2016). According to Ratcliffe (2016), these criteria may require a substantial cultural change that is supportive of greater autonomy for lower-ranking officers. That said, problem-oriented policing has had an important role in the emergence of ILP as it helped to lay the foundation within law enforcement, particularly among management, that crime analysis can play a critical role in the formulation of operational strategies (Ratcliffe 2016).

CompStat, which in many ways extends from problem-oriented policing, aims to hold decision-makers accountable by intensely monitoring and analysing crime trends (Carter and Carter 2009, p. 320). An initiative of the New York City Police Department, CompStat was positively associated with a swift reduction in crime rates immediately following its introduction, and was consequently adopted by law enforcement agencies around the world (Vito et al. 2017). It was believed that making managers within law enforcement agencies accountable would make them more inclined to use the intelligence available to them and subsequently develop more effective crime reduction strategies. However, questions have been raised about the effectiveness of CompStat. For example, in New York City, and many other cities in the US, crime rates had already been dropping for several years before CompStat was introduced (Levitt 2004). Levitt (2004, p. 173) argued that other factors are likely to have had a greater impact on the reduction in crime within New York City, including a 45 per cent increase in the size of the police force from 1991 to 2001, three times more than the national average. It has also been noted that CompStat is largely orientated towards addressing only street crime (Ratcliffe 2016). Despite this, some of the key principles of CompStat, including the importance of using intelligence to guide decision-making, particularly at the managerial level, have been incorporated into the latest framework, ILP.

ILP (also called intelligence-driven policing) has been widely adopted in many countries, including the US, United Kingdom (UK), Canada, Australia and New Zealand (Ratcliffe 2016). ILP draws on elements of the aforementioned frameworks, in particular problem-oriented policing and CompStat, and aims to make decision-making analysis-driven. Furthermore, ILP seeks to move away from a 'reactive' or 'prosecution-directed mode' of policing to a more 'proactive' style of crime prevention (Innes et al. 2005, p. 41; Innes and Sheptycki 2004, p. 1). According to Ratcliffe (2016, p. 66), one of the leading authors on ILP, it can be defined as follows:

> Intelligence-led policing emphasises analysis and intelligence as pivotal to an objective, decision-making framework that prioritises crime hot spots, repeat victims, prolific offenders and criminal groups. It facilitates crime and harm reduction, disruption and prevention through strategic and tactical management, deployment, and enforcement.[1]

---

[1] ILP has been defined and conceptualised differently by Carter and Carter (2009). This study has adopted the version of ILP put forward by Ratcliffe (2016) for two reasons. First, the initial criticism and apparent differences between the two versions of ILP suggested by Carter (2013) have largely been addressed in updated versions of Ratcliffe's approach (Ratcliffe 2016), meaning the two are hard to distinguish. Secondly, Ratcliffe's (2016, p. 81) 3-I model (examined later in the chapter), which depicts the main components of ILP, was reportedly adapted from a diagram used

It differs from the previous law enforcement frameworks in several ways. In contrast with problem-oriented policing, which has a strong focus on tactical intelligence, ILP is concerned with both tactical and strategic intelligence. Tactical intelligence can be defined as an 'intelligence product supporting front line units in taking case-specific action to achieve compliance or enforcement objectives' (Innes and Sheptycki 2004, p. 7). An example would be information about the specific location of a drug manufacturing site. Unlike tactical intelligence, where a definition has been largely agreed upon (Coyne and Bell 2011a), a shared definition of strategic intelligence remains elusive (Innes and Sheptycki 2004). Therefore, this study will adopt a relatively simple definition. Strategic intelligence can be defined as an attempt 'to provide insight and understanding, and make a contribution to broad strategies, policies and resources' (Ratcliffe 2016, p. 74).[2] While both CompStat and ILP are strategically driven, CompStat is focused primarily on crime hot spots, predominantly street crime (such as robbery). ILP is seen as a much broader framework that covers the diverse range of policing activities, including tasks like traffic accident reduction (Ratcliffe 2016). As such, ILP is regarded as a 'business model' that places 'crime intelligence' at the forefront of managerial decisions concerning the prevention and control of crime (Guidette and Martinelli 2009, p. 132; Ratcliffe 2016, p. 89). Crime intelligence can be defined as:

> Analysed information that blends data from crime analysis of crime patterns and hot spots and criminal intelligence drawn from the behaviour of offenders. Here the term *crime intelligence* is used to reflect a realisation that good intelligence stems not only from knowledge about offenders

---

by the Australian Federal Police (AFP). Given that this study is focused on policing within Australia it is appropriate that Ratcliffe's version is followed.

[2] While much of the intelligence literature defines intelligence on these two 'planes of operation' (Ratcliffe 2016, p. 74), others place a third plane, *operational intelligence*, between strategic and tactical intelligence (see Aldrich 2009; Carter 2009; Ratcliffe 2016; Walsh 2011). Operational intelligence can be defined as 'supporting area commanders and regional operational commanders in planning crime reduction activity and deploying resources to achieve operational objectives' (Ratcliffe 2016, p. 74).

(criminal intelligence) but also about crime events (crime analysis). (Ratcliffe 2016, p. 65)[3]

Ratcliffe (2016) and others (Cope 2004; Darroch and Mazerolle 2013; Phillips 2012; Sanders et al. 2015) have suggested that embedding the principles of ILP in law enforcement agencies can be challenging for a number of reasons. These include a misconception that ILP only relates to covert activity rather than a 'managerial process for prioritising resource allocation', a concern that increased proactive policing will impinge upon civil liberties, resource constraints and a conservative police culture (Ratcliffe 2016, p. 176). Nevertheless, the rise in popularity of ILP is likely attributable to several factors, foremost of which is the shift towards 'disruption' as a strategic intervention within the proactive model of policing (Innes and Sheptycki 2004). While disruption is not necessarily a new strategy—it has indeed been a core approach for security intelligence agencies for some time—there has been a growing shift towards its use by law enforcement agencies (Innes and Sheptycki 2004). Disruption refers to a strategy employed by law enforcement and security agencies, whereby they take various courses of action towards criminal networks in an effort to make it as difficult as possible for them to continue with their illegal activities (Innes and Sheptycki 2004, p. 13). This can include the removal of actors from a network, such as arresting key individuals (Innes and Sheptycki 2004; Morselli and Petit 2007), financial intervention like the targeting of unexplained wealth or freezing of funds (Bell 2003; Murray 2013), and disrupting supplies such as the monitoring of precursor chemicals required for manufacturing illicit drugs (Cunningham and Liu 2005; McKetin et al. 2011). The expanding use of disruption strategies has been driven, in part, by the apparent advantages of a disruption approach over the traditional prosecutorial aims that have long been central to law enforcement frameworks. For example, an increased police

---

[3] Outside of the US, the distinction between crime analysis and criminal intelligence is largely non-existent. Furthermore, as will be seen in Chap. 2, while much of the SNA literature focuses on criminal offenders (which would come under 'criminal intelligence'), SNA has also been applied to offender locations (Bichler et al. 2014; Gupta 2011), which would fall under 'crime analysis'. Therefore, following Ratcliffe (2016), this study will adopt the all-encompassing term of *crime intelligence*.

presence in areas known to be hot spots for the distribution of illicit drugs may disrupt the criminality in that area without the involvement of the wider criminal justice system, such as the courts. However, criminological research has shown that such strategies risk simply 'displacing' the crime elsewhere (Lazzati and Menichini 2016). Another reported capability of disruption is that it can allow law enforcement agencies to target offenders for offences other than their 'main' criminality (Innes and Sheptycki 2004, pp. 14–15), such as charging a drug dealer for repeat traffic infringements or tax violations, with a view to disrupting the drug-related activity. Finally, disruption is seen as a way of causing problems for criminal networks without the need to target the entire network, a task which is often very difficult (Décary-Hétu and Dupont 2012). By targeting important individuals within criminal groups, it is believed that different types of disruption can occur, ranging from increased difficulty in the flow of information and resources to the total fragmentation of such groups.

Crime intelligence is critical to achieving the objectives of ILP, including the disruption of criminal networks. It is therefore necessary to examine in greater detail the role of intelligence within the policing framework of ILP. This will, in turn, allow for a clearer understanding of where SNA fits within crime intelligence.

The 3-I Model and Crime Intelligence

There have been many attempts to conceptualise the intelligence process, including: the intelligence cycle; the Scan, Analyse, Respond and Assess (or SARA) model; the fractal intelligence model and more recently the 3-I model (Hawley and Marden 2006; Ratcliffe 2016; Walsh 2011).[4] Developed

---

[4] There are numerous versions of the intelligence cycle; however, they broadly follow the same six stages: planning, collection, collation and evaluation, analysis, dissemination and feedback (Ratcliffe 2016). The SARA model adopts a different theoretical approach whereby analysts *scan* for reoccurring crime problems; *analyse* these problems to identify underlying causes; determine what *responses* should be used to address the problem and *assess* the effectiveness of the employed responses (Ratcliffe 2016). The fractal intelligence model is similar to the intelligence cycle in that it involves the same processes. Where it differs is that it 'represents the intelligence process as a

by Ratcliffe (2016), the 3-I model provides a framework for understanding the role of crime intelligence within ILP.[5] The 3-I model is a relatively simple way of conceptualising how ILP functions. It is not a model of intelligence *per se*, but rather seeks to clearly outline the role of intelligence within the ILP business model. Ratcliffe (2016, p. 83) argued that the 3-I model is better than the aforementioned models of intelligence at demonstrating the 'big picture environment of the law enforcement world' in that it shows clearly where both the intelligence analyst and the decision-maker (the client) fit within an ILP paradigm. In other models, such as the intelligence cycle, decision-makers are largely absent, suggesting analysts' work is separate from the 'action component of policing' (Ratcliffe 2016, p. 83). In contrast, the 3-I model requires that the analyst influence decision-makers, tying the production of intelligence and decision-making together.

The 3-I model is depicted as a triangle with 'criminal environment', 'crime intelligence analysis' and 'decision-maker' each at one point of the triangle respectively. Each side of the triangle then consists of one of three elements: *interpreting* the criminal environment, *influencing* decision-makers and having an *impact* on the crime. Although interpreting the criminal environment is 'one of three symbiotic conceptual parts' that comprise ILP, decisions made at this stage will have a disproportionate impact on the rest of the model (Ratcliffe 2016, p. 86). At this stage, there is a unidirectional arrow from *crime intelligence analysis* to the *criminal environment*. Some may take issue with the direction of this arrow as it involves analysts having to obtain information from numerous sources.

---

potentially unlimited number of interrelated, overlapping intelligence processes, rather than a set of neat sequential phases as depicted normally in the intelligence cycle' (Walsh 2011, p. 65).

[5] It is important to briefly note why the intelligence cycle, arguably the most popular model of intelligence, has not been used. Although the intelligence cycle has been critical to the study and application of intelligence since World War Two (Phythian 2013a), to the point where it has become an almost 'theological concept' whose validity is rarely questioned (Clarke 2013, p. 5), there is growing recognition of its many limitations (Hulnick 2006; Phythian 2013b; Ratcliffe 2016; Sheptycki 2013; Warner 2013). The most common criticism of the intelligence cycle is that in reality the process of producing intelligence is not as rigid as it is depicted in the model. Analysts more often than not are jumping back and forth between the different stages of the cycle, often undertaking several stages simultaneously (Hulnick 2006; Ratcliffe 2016). A further criticism of the intelligence cycle is how it essentially views intelligence in isolation, paying no consideration to the broader law enforcement or security environment in which it sits. This is particularly important when examining intelligence within ILP, where both *intelligence* and *policing* should be of equal importance (Ratcliffe 2016). It is for these reasons that this study has used the 3-I model.

The reason for this, as Ratcliffe (2016, p. 78) suggested, is that it is only in an 'intelligence utopia' that analysts send out information requests that are promptly returned by patrol officers and other analysts (a push model). A more accurate reflection of the policing environment consists of analysts actively seeking out intelligence from a variety of sources (a pull model). The second 'I', influence, runs from *criminal intelligence analysis* to *decision-makers*. One of the key aims of the 3-I model is to highlight to analysts that while interpreting the criminal environment is critical, so too is influencing the decision-makers 'who have the resources and capacity to have an impact on the criminal environment' (Ratcliffe 2016, p. 110). The third 'I', impact, runs from the *decision-maker* to the *criminal environment*. This is a key difference from other models, such as the intelligence cycle, which often see the creation of an intelligence product and its dissemination as the conclusion of this process. According to the 3-I model, this only occurs once attempts have been made to actually reduce criminality (Ratcliffe 2016).[6]

At the heart of the 3-I model is crime intelligence, which in turn utilises numerous analytical and investigative methods in an effort to accurately interpret the criminal environment. Over the past decade in particular these methods have been evolving quickly. For example, Heuer et al. (2010) suggested there are several hundred analytical techniques available to analysts. The National Intelligence Model, a UK policy that aims to implement the principles of ILP, encourages the use of nine categories of analytical tools and products. These include: crime pattern analysis, criminal business profiles, risk analysis and network analysis (NCIS 2000). Network analysis in particular has grown in popularity with both researchers and practitioners (Bouchard and Amirault 2013; Morselli 2014; Mullins 2012b). Network analysis is not a methodology itself but a broad all-encompassing category of tools that can refer to

---

[6] It should be noted that police leaders with greater experience are more likely to take an active role in the intelligence process by providing supervision and guidance to analysts (Ratcliffe 2016). Therefore, in police organisations or individual units with mature decision-making systems, there will in fact be a fourth 'I'—intent—running from *decision-maker* to *crime intelligence analysis* (opposite direction of influence), thus creating the 4-I model. For the purposes of this study and to be consistent with other literature (Walsh 2011), it will simply be referred to by its more common name, the 3-I model.

criminal network analysis, link analysis, visual link analysis, statistical link analysis, dynamic network analysis and SNA (Carley 2006; Duval et al. 2010; Hutchins and Benham-Hutchins 2010). At times these approaches are viewed as independent, while at other times they are used interchangeably and are simply referred to as network analysis (Burcher and Whelan 2015; Klerks 1999). The focus of this study, however, is specifically on SNA and its unique characteristics. SNA is considered to be both a theoretical and methodological approach to understanding social structures (Papachristos 2014). By examining the role of SNA within crime intelligence, particularly within operational environments, this study makes an original contribution to an area of the network analysis literature that has so far received little attention (Duijn and Klerks 2014; Johnson and Reitzal 2011).

Networks and Social Network Analysis

Networks are simply a way of thinking about social systems with a particular focus on 'the relationships among entities that make up the system' (Borgatti et al. 2013, p. 1). However, the term 'network' is often used in a variety of ways. It can be used as a metaphor (e.g., the idea that we live in a 'network society') (Castells 2010), as a unit of analysis (such as referring to the structure of an organisation), and as a method of analysis (Whelan 2012). It is the last two that are of interest to this study, in particular the concept of 'network' as a methodology. When conducting network analysis, specifically SNA, a network is defined as a set of 'actors'[7] that may or may not have 'relationships' (Borgatti et al. 2013). Actors can be people, groups or organisations, for example. Relationships can be of any type, including kinship, friendship, religious and economic connections (Bright et al. 2015b; Carley et al. 2003). Actors and relationships

---

[7] SNA has mathematical foundations whereby a network is conceptualised using a graph. As Borgatti et al. (2013) explained, the term 'graph' does not mean a diagram but a mathematical object. A graph consists of vertices (points in the graph) connected by edges (lines in the graph). However, within the SNA field there is an array of terminology that is used interchangeably. Relationships, connections, ties, links and lines are all terms for the edges in a network; while individuals, actors and nodes all refer to the vertices in a network (Borgatti et al. 2013). Because this study is focused on *social* networks and not networks containing inanimate objects, 'relationships' (the edges) and 'actors' (the vertices) are used as the preferred terminology.

both have what is referred to as 'attributes' (Borgatti et al. 2013). This can include relatively basic biographical data about actors, for example their age and sex, to more complex attributes, such as their individual skill set. For relationships, this can include the 'frequency' (such as how often two actors communicate) and 'substance' (e.g., what is being discussed when they communicate) of the connections in a network (Koschade 2006). The relative strength of a relationship (referred to as link weightings) can also be included in an analysis (see Chap. 4).

To conduct SNA, information is collected on a set of actors, including information on the existence of relationships and the characteristics of those relationships (hereafter simply 'relational data'). These data are combined with graph theory and a number of mathematical computations or metrics (Borgatti et al. 2013). There are two outputs of SNA: a link diagram (or visual representation of a network) and the results of a number of different mathematical computations. The mathematical computations used in SNA are what separate it from other forms of analysis such as 'link analysis', which simply involves determining who is connected to whom (van der Hulst 2009). The computations inherent in SNA provide a degree of methodological rigour and objectivity to the analysis of social networks (Berlusconi 2013; Lampe 2009; Mainas 2012). A commonly used mathematical computation is 'betweenness centrality', a measure of the shortest path between two actors that is often used to identify 'brokers' (Borgatti et al. 2013). High betweenness centrality is considered an indication of an actor's critical importance as they will likely have a level of control over the flow of information and resources in a network (Morselli 2010). It is believed that such mathematical computations can identify patterns in the relationships of a network and the implications of these relationships for the network as a whole (Carrington et al. 2005; Wasserman and Faust 1994).

By focusing on the relationships between actors it is argued that SNA enhances crime intelligence, and is aligned with the proactive and disruption-oriented principles of ILP. SNA can assist law enforcement in the development of disruption strategies by identifying 'key players'[8] and

---

[8] According to Bouchard and Nash (2015, p. 55) what constitutes a 'key player' or a 'key actor' from those who can be ignored depends on two points: the objectives and priorities of law enforce-

points of vulnerability in a network (van der Hulst 2009). SNA can detect actors with similar positions in a network (or 'role equivalence') and therefore can identify not only key actors but also their likely 'successors' if they are removed (e.g., by arrest) (van der Hulst 2009, p. 105). Removal of key actors and those who are similarly positioned is likely to cause greater disruption to the targeted network (Koschade 2006). SNA can also be used to identify suitable informants, such as those who are largely unknown to the police but have knowledge of a targeted network (Duijn and Klerks 2014). Finally, SNA can be used to guide investigations by suggesting where resources, such as surveillance, should be focused (Schwartz and Rouselle 2009), as well as where undercover officers might best be positioned within a network (Bright et al. 2017).

Although there has been considerable interest in the application of SNA to criminal networks, we know almost nothing about its use by those who arguably stand to benefit most from its reported capabilities, intelligence analysts. There have been very few studies that have examined the use of SNA in operational law enforcement environments (Duijn and Klerks 2014; Johnson and Reitzal 2011). This study is designed to address this gap in our understanding by conducting in-depth qualitative interviews with intelligence analysts from two Australian state law enforcement agencies.

Research Design

The discipline of criminology has overwhelmingly relied on quantitative research. Copes et al. (2016) suggested that no more than one in ten articles published in criminology and criminal justice journals contain qualitative data. However, as the authors note, this appears to be changing, with increasing numbers looking to publish qualitative research. Unlike quantitative research, which tends to be 'prescribed, algorithmic, and linear', qualitative research generally involves methods that are

---

ment, and the ability of the network to recover. Actors can be valuable for a variety of reasons, including the fact that they have a large number of relationships in the targeted network, they are in brokerage positions, or that they bring unique resources to the network (such as social, human or financial capital) (Bouchard and Nash 2015).

'eclectic, heuristic, and holistic' (Saldana 2011, p. 30). Furthermore, it involves developing 'concepts, insights, and understandings from patterns in the data rather than collecting data to assess preconceived models, hypotheses, or theories' (Taylor et al. 2016, p. 18). Therefore, qualitative research can provide detailed insight into what can be a highly complex phenomenon (Ritchie and Lewis 2003). The exploratory nature of this study is enhanced by the use of qualitative methods, which facilitate a rich understanding of the role of SNA in operational environments, and in particular the types of challenges law enforcement analysts face when looking to apply SNA to criminal networks.

The research design adopted for this study involved the use of semi-structured interviews with intelligence analysts, as this format provided the best opportunity for gaining in-depth insight into the value of SNA as an investigative tool in operational environments.[9] The value of semi-structured interviews has been well documented (Atkinson and Delamont 2010; Galletta 2013; Ritchie and Lewis 2003). Arguably the greatest strength of semi-structured interviews is that there is sufficient structure to address key elements of a research question, but the interviews are also sufficiently flexible to allow research participants to provide new insight into the topic under investigation (Galletta 2013).

The interviews were conducted with intelligence analysts from two Australian state law enforcement agencies, Victoria Police and New South Wales Police Force.[10] Victoria Police and New South Wales Police Force were specifically selected for two reasons. First, they are the two largest law enforcement agencies in Australia. Victoria Police services a population of just under 6.4 million people across 237,639 square kilometres, has a staff of approximately 19,600 and an annual budget of 3 billion (Victoria Police 2019). New South Wales Police Force services just over 7.6 million people across 800,642 square kilometres, has a staff of approximately 21,000 and an annual budget of 3.6 billion (NSWPF 2019). Law

---

[9] Ritchie and Lewis (2003, p. 111) note that there is a great deal of inconsistency in the use of terms like 'semi-structured interviews', with some referring to it as 'in-depth' interviewing and even 'open-ended survey interviews'. Maxfield and Babbie (2011, p. 283) refer to semi-structured interviews as 'specialized interviewing'.

[10] The personal views of participants presented in this book do not represent the views of the organisation they work for.

enforcement in Australia is state-based, meaning Victoria Police and New South Wales Police Force service not only large municipalities, but also small regional towns. The second reason these organisations were selected is that both follow, at least in principle, the policing paradigm of ILP (Mullane 2015; Victoria Police 2014). This is critical as this study seeks to better understand the role of SNA within ILP. The in-depth interviews with Victoria Police intelligence analysts took place between September 2014 and January 2016 at general regional and metropolitan police stations. The interviews with New South Wales Police Force took place over two days in December 2015 at their police headquarters and a metropolitan station. In accordance with the research agreements with each organisation the names of the participants were redacted, and each participant was given a randomly assigned numerical pseudonym (e.g., Analyst No. 1).

The analysts came from a variety of units, with many having experience in both regional intelligence divisions that are primarily concerned with local crime, and specialist intelligence units/taskforces that are focused on particular groups (such as outlaw motorcycle gangs) or specific crime problems (e.g., 'the drug squad'). The level of analytical experience varied among research participants, ranging from just 2 years up to 25 years. However, many had experience in other positions at their agency prior to becoming analysts, including as front-line officers ($n = 19$). There were also eight analysts in total who were 'unsworn' members of their organisation.[11] As part of becoming an intelligence analyst, each participant had completed at least one internal analyst training programme, with the more experienced analysts having completed multiple courses as they had been updated over the years ($n = 19$). Most interviewees had also undertaken a number of short courses (1–2 days) that often focused on one software program or system. Twelve analysts had also obtained tertiary qualifications, both outside their field (in disciplines such as politics) and directly related to intelligence analysis (including some who had completed postgraduate studies applying SNA to criminal networks). With regard to specific SNA training, New South Wales Police Force had

---

[11] Sworn officers are police officers that have gone through the requisite training and have the capacity to use the associated powers, such as the ability to arrest citizens. Unsworn officers are still members of the police force but are in civilian roles. Intelligence analyst positions are increasingly being filled by unsworn officers (Cope 2004; Evans and Kebbell 2012).

recently added a new section to their internal training course for analysts that covered the 'basics' of SNA, although not all of those who were interviewed had completed this training as they were not new recruits. They had also run several workshops on the application of SNA to outline its capabilities. At the time of this research, Victoria Police did not have a specific SNA course, yet as part of their internal training programme for analysts they receive training on Analyst Notebook, analytical software which includes SNA functionality.[12]

Once the interviews were completed the audio was transcribed and entered into QSR NVivo 11,[13] where a thematic analysis was undertaken. A thematic analysis 'is used to classify and organise data according to key themes, concepts and emergent categories' (Ritchie and Lewis 2003, p. 220) and according to Guest MacQueen and Namey (2014, p. 10) is 'useful in capturing the complexities of meaning within a textual data set'. For this study, regularly used 'quantitative descriptors' (e.g., 'all', 'most', 'some' and 'several') are employed to give some indication of what are the more common themes in the data (Guest et al. 2014, p. 157). However, because this study used both purposive and snowball sampling the participants are not necessarily representative, meaning that these descriptors cannot be generalised either within or beyond the agencies involved. Consistent with the qualitative approach adopted for this study, quotations from participants are presented to highlight common themes. These quotes were selected based on their informative nature and their representativeness of the themes being discussed. It should be noted that reports presenting qualitative data are often criticised for having 'cherry-picked' quotes (Guest et al. 2014, p. 99). One method to counteract this concern is to present 'negative cases', instances where the views of one or two participants go against the prevailing view or where a particular issue has only been raised by one or two participants. Therefore, to help

---

[12] When reporting qualitative data, it is common practice to provide a slightly more in-depth description of the research participants (see Guest et al. 2014). For example, it would have been potentially useful to have a more detailed description of each analyst's experience. However, due to the topic under investigation and the profession from which the participants come, a balance had to be struck between providing enough contextual detail necessary for the interpretation of the research findings and adhering to the confidentiality clause stipulated in the research agreement with each organisation.

[13] QSR NVivo 11 is software that allows for the analysis of unstructured qualitative data.

improve the validity of the data contained in this study, negative cases are presented throughout.

It should be noted that there are several limitations with the data. Because participants come from only two state law enforcement agencies and the sample size is relatively small, the research is not necessarily representative. As such, any generalisations made based upon the findings of this study should be considered in light of these data limitations. Furthermore, while the focus of this study is specifically on the use of SNA within ILP, law enforcement agencies work extremely closely with national security and intelligence agencies, particularly when it involves counter-terrorism (see Chap. 2). In the present study, federal agencies are not represented, further limiting the generalisability of the findings. There is also a concern with the interview data that there may be a difference in what participants say compared with what they truly think and the actions they take (Whelan and Molnar 2017). This is particularly true of interviews involving participants from professions who are understandably secretive, such as law enforcement. Despite these limitations, the data presented in this book provides a unique insight into the application of SNA with ILP environments, and in particular the challenges analysts have faced when applying SNA to criminal networks. This is an area of research that has received almost no attention from scholars of intelligence or SNA.

Book Structure

Chapter 2 provides a review of the existing SNA literature. The chapter begins by examining the key theories that underpin SNA and how they have been critical to its application. Attention then turns to the development of SNA in law enforcement, focusing on the 'three generations' of network analysis development outlined by Klerks (1999). The chapter then examines the different types of criminal networks that SNA has been applied to, what it has been able to reveal about these groups and the implications of this for law enforcement. Following this, the main challenges and limitations of applying SNA to criminal networks are explored. It is argued that in order to understand the prospects of SNA as an investigative tool we must understand the challenges analysts face when applying it to criminal networks. The chapter concludes by examining what are regarded as the primary gaps within the SNA literature, where it is argued that we know almost nothing about its use within operational environments.

Chapter 3 focuses on whether and how intelligence analysts are using SNA in operational environments. This chapter uses Klerks' (1999) three 'generations' of network analysis development as a reference point. It is necessary to examine the first two generations of network analysis to understand why in some instances they are still being used by intelligence analysts. The third generation of network analysis, or SNA, is examined in much greater detail. The chapter focuses on the different ways in which SNA is being used by those interviewed, including the detection of network vulnerabilities, the identification of further avenues of enquiry, the use of link and attribute weightings and the difficulty of determining at what stage of the investigation it should be applied.

Chapter 4 examines the 'characteristics of criminal networks' introduced by Sparrow (1991), which have been heavily cited in more recent literature (Duijn and Klerks 2014; Malm et al. 2008; Yuan et al. 2013). These characteristics or challenges include the fact that criminal databases can be incredibly large, that crime data tends to be incomplete, that the boundaries of a network are often 'fuzzy' and that social networks are dynamic, meaning the relationships and actors that make up a network are constantly changing. Several other 'data challenges' have been recognised alongside incompleteness of criminal network data, including *incorrectness*, *inconsistences* and *data transformation* (Morris and Deckro 2013; Xu and Chen 2005). These data challenges are also examined.

The next three chapters examine what has been termed the 'organisational characteristics of law enforcement agencies' (Burcher and Whelan 2017, p. 1), including *Investigative Focus*; *Working Relationships* and *IT Software, Systems and Training*. It was evident from interviewees that the organisational environment in which they operate can impact on the utilising of SNA as an investigative tool. Chapter 5 examines investigative focus, which refers to how the objectives and priorities of an investigation, and more broadly that of the unit/taskforce that analysts are embedded in, impacts on how SNA is used and the opportunities analysts have to apply it. Chapter 6 explores how key working relationships, those between analysts and detectives, and analysts and managers, can impact the ability of analysts to apply SNA. Chapter 7 examines the challenges associated with IT software, systems and training that are critical to the application of SNA. These characteristics are likely to be found in varying degrees within every law enforcement agency (Carter 2009; Ratcliffe 2005, 2016; Sheptycki 2004).

The final chapter (Chap. 8) provides a discussion of the main findings and a conclusion to this study by outlining the primary contributions that have been made to the intelligence and SNA literature. In particular, the chapter highlights key lessons for both researchers and practitioners in relation to how they apply SNA to criminal networks. Finally, this chapter outlines the limitations of this study and several critical areas that should be the focus of future research.

References

R.J. Aldrich, US-European intelligence co-operation on counter-terrorism: low politics and compulsion. Br. J. Polit. Int. Rel. **11**(1), 122–139 (2009)

J. Arquilla, To build a network. Prism **4**(1), 22–33 (2014)

P. Atkinson, S. Delamont, *SAGE qualitative research methods* (SAGE Research Methods, 2010). http://methods.sagepub.com/book/sage-qualitative-research-methods. Accessed 29 April 2017

L. Ball, Automating social network analysis: a power tool for counter-terrorism. Security J. **29**(2), 147–168 (2016)

R.E. Bell, The confiscation, forfeiture and disruption of terrorist finances. J. Money Laundering Control **7**(2), 105–125 (2003)

G. Berlusconi, Do all the pieces matter? assessing the reliability of law enforcement data sources for the network analysis of wire taps. Global Crime **14**(1), 61–81 (2013)

G. Bichler, A. Malm, J. Enriquez, Magnetic facilities: identifying key juvenile convergence places with social network analysis. Crime Delinq. **60**(7), 971–998 (2014)

S. Borgatti, M. Everett, J.C. Johnson, *Analyzing social networks* (SAGE Publications, London, 2013)

S.P. Borgatti, A. Mehra, D.J. Brass, G. Labianca, Network analysis in the social sciences. Science **323**(5916), 892–895 (2009)

M. Bouchard, J. Amirault, Advances in research on illicit networks. Global Crime **14**(2–3), 119–122 (2013)

M. Bouchard, R. Nash, Researching terrorism and counter-terrorism through a network lens, in *Social networks, terrorism, and counter-terrorism: radical and connected*, ed. by M. Bouchard, (Routledge, New York, 2015), pp. 48–60

D. Bright, C. Greenhill, T. Britz, A. Ritter, C. Morselli, Criminal network vulnerabilities and adaptations. Global Crime **18**(4), 424–441 (2017)

D.A. Bright, C. Greenhill, M. Reynolds, A. Ritter, C. Morselli, The use of actor-level attributes and centrality measures to identify key actors: a case study of an Australian drug trafficking network. J. Contemp. Crim. Justice **31**(3), 262–278 (2015a)

D.A. Bright, C. Greenhill, A. Ritter, C. Morselli, Networks within networks: using multiple link types to examine network structure and identify key actors in a drug trafficking operation. Global Crime **16**(3), 1–19 (2015b)

D.A. Bright, C.E. Hughes, J. Chalmers, Illuminating dark networks: a social network analysis of an Australian drug trafficking syndicate. Crime Law Soc. Chang. **57**(2), 151–176 (2012)

J.-P. Brodeur, B. Dupont, Knowledge workers or "knowledge" workers? Polic. Soc. **16**(1), 7–26 (2006)

M. Burcher, C. Whelan, Social network analysis and small group 'dark' networks: an analysis of the London bombers and the problem of 'fuzzy' boundaries. Global Crime **16**(2), 104–122 (2015)

M. Burcher, C. Whelan, Social network analysis as a tool for criminal intelligence: understanding its potential from the perspectives of intelligence analysts. Trends. Org. Crime **21**(3), 278–294 (2017)

K.M. Carley, Destabilization of covert networks. Comput. Math. Org. Theor. **12**(1), 51–66 (2006)

K.M. Carley, M. Dombroski, M. Tsvetovat, J. Reminga, N. Kamneva, Destabilizing dynamic covert networks', in *Paper presented to Proceedings of the 8th International Command and Control Research and Technology Symposium*, (National Defense War College, Washington, DC, 2003)

P.J. Carrington, J. Scott, S. Wasserman, *Models and methods in social network analysis* (Cambridge University Press, Cambridge, 2005)

D.L. Carter, *Law enforcement intelligence: a guide for state, local, and tribal law enforcement agencies* (2009), No. 24 July 2012. https://it.ojp.gov/documents/d/e050919201-IntelGuide_web.pdf. Accessed 21 August 2018

D.L. Carter, J.G. Carter, Intelligence-led policing: conceptual and functional considerations for public policy. Crim. Justice Policy Rev. **20**(3), 310–325 (2009)

J.G. Carter, *Intelligence-led policing: a policing innovation* (LFB Scholarly Publishing LLC, El Paso, 2013)

M. Castells, *The network society* (Edward Elgar Publishing, Cheltenham, UK, 2004)

M. Castells, *The rise of the network society*, vol 1 (Wiley-Blackwell, Chichester, UK, 2010)

R.M. Clarke, *Intelligence analysis: a target-centric approach*, 4th edn. (CQ Press, California, 2013)

N. Cope, Intelligence led policing or policing led intelligence? Br. J. Criminol. **44**(2), 188–203 (2004)

H. Copes, R. Tewksbury, S. Sandberg, Publishing qualitative research in criminology and criminal justice journals. J. Criminal Justice Educ. **27**(1), 121–139 (2016)

J.W. Coyne, P. Bell, The role of strategic intelligence in anticipating transnational organised crime. Int. J. Law Crime Justice **39**(1), 60–78 (2011a)

J.W. Coyne, P. Bell, Strategic intelligence in law enforcement: a review. J. Polic. Intell. Counter Terrorism **6**(1), 23–39 (2011b)

J.K. Cunningham, L.-M. Liu, Impacts of federal precursor chemical regulations on methamphetamine arrests. Addiction **100**(4), 479–488 (2005)

S. Darroch, L. Mazerolle, Intelligence-led policing: a comparative analysis of organizational factors influencing innovation uptake. Police Q. **16**(1), 3–37 (2013)

D. Décary-Hétu, B. Dupont, The social network of hackers. Global Crime **13**(3), 160–175 (2012)

P.A.C. Duijn, P.P.H.M. Klerks, Social network analysis applied to criminal networks: recent developments in Dutch law enforcement, in *Networks and network analysis for defence and security*, ed. by A. J. Masys, (Springer, Heidelberg, 2014), pp. 121–159

R.D. Duval, K. Christensen, A. Spahiu, *Bootstrapping a terrorist network*, Paper presented to Political Networks Conference, Southern Illinois University Carbondale, May 2010. http://opensiuc.lib.siu.edu/cgi/viewcontent.cgi?article=1017&context=pnconfs_2010

J.M. Evans, M.R. Kebbell, The effective analyst: a study of what makes an effective crime and intelligence analyst. Polic. Soc. **22**(3), 204–219 (2012)

H. Fruhling, The impact of international models in Latin America: the case of community policing. Police Pract. Res. **8**(2), 125–144 (2007)

A. Galletta, *Mastering the semi-structured interview and beyond: from research design to analysis and publication* (New York University Press, New York, 2013)

C. Gill, D. Weisburd, C.W. Telep, Z. Vitter, T. Bennett, Community-oriented policing to reduce crime, disorder and fear and increase satisfaction and legitimacy among citizens: a systematic review. J. Exp. Criminol. **10**(4), 399–428 (2014)

H. Goldstein, Improving policing: a problem-oriented approach. Crime Delinq. **25**(2), 236–258 (1979)

G. Guest, K.M. MacQueen, E.E. Namey, *Applied thematic analysis* (Sage Publications, Thousand Oaks, CA, 2014)

R. Guidette, T.J. Martinelli, Intelligence-led policing: strategic framework. Police Chief **76**(10), 132–136 (2009)

R. Gupta, *Utilizing network analysis to identify critical vulnerability points in infrastructure and explain terrorist target selection*, Master of Arts in Security Studies thesis, Georgetown University, 2011

W.R. Harper, D.H. Harris, The application of link analysis to police intelligence. Hum. Factors **17**(2), 157–164 (1975)

R.V. Hauck, H. Atabakhsh, P. Ongvasith, H. Gupta, H. Chen, Using Coplink to analyze criminal-justice data. Computer **35**(3), 30–37 (2002)

M.S. Hawley, B.C. Marden, FIM: a business information system for intelligence. Int. J. Intell. Counterintell. **19**(3), 443–455 (2006)

J. Heuer, J. Richards, R.H. Pherson, *Structured analytic techniques for intelligence analysis* (CQ Press, Washington, DC, 2010)

A.S. Hulnick, What's wrong with the intelligence cycle. Intell. Nat. Secur. **21**(6), 959–979 (2006)

C.E. Hutchins, M. Benham-Hutchins, Hiding in plain sight: criminal network analysis. Comput. Math. Org. Theor. **16**(1), 89–111 (2010)

M. Innes, N. Fielding, N. Cope, The appliance of science? The theory and practice of crime intelligence analysis. Br. J. Criminol. **45**(1), 39–57 (2005)

M. Innes, J. Sheptycki, From detection to disruption: intelligence and the changing logic of police crime control in the United Kingdom. Int. Criminal Justice Rev. **14**(1), 1–24 (2004)

J.A. Johnson, J.D. Reitzal, *Social network analysis in an operational environment: defining the utility of a network approach for crime analysis using the Richmond City Police Department as a case study* (2011). http://www.coginta.org/en/document/policy_working_paper_series?page=3. Accessed 8 August 2012

P. Klerks, The network paradigm applied to criminal organisations: theoretical nitpicking or relevant doctrine for investigators? Recent developments in the Netherlands. Connections **24**(3), 53–65 (1999)

S. Koschade, A social network analysis of Jemaah Islamiyah: the applications to counterterrorism and intelligence. Stud. Conflict Terrorism **29**(6), 559–575 (2006)

V. Krebs, Mapping networks of terrorist cells. Connections **24**(3), 43–52 (2002)

K. Lampe, Human capital and social capital in criminal networks: introduction to the special issue on the 7th Blankensee Colloquium. Trends. Org. Crime **12**(2), 93–100 (2009)

N. Lazzati, A.A. Menichini, Hot spot policing: a study of place-based strategies for crime prevention. South. Econ. J. **82**(3), 893–913 (2016)

S.D. Levitt, Understanding why crime fell in the 1990s: four factors that explain the decline and six that do not. J. Econ. Perspect. **18**(1), 163–190 (2004)

J. Liederbach, E.J. Fritsch, D.L. Carter, A. Bannister, Exploring the limits of collaboration in community orientated policing. Polic. Int. J. Police Strategies Manage. **31**(1), 271–291 (2008)

E.D. Mainas, The analysis of criminal and terrorist organisations as social network structures: a quasi-experimental study. Int. J. Police Sci. Manage. **14**(3), 264–283 (2012)

A. Malm, J.B. Kinney, N.R. Pollard, Social network and distance correlates of criminal associates involved in illicit drug production. Security J. **21**(1–2), 77–94 (2008)

M.G. Maxfield, E.R. Babbie, *Research methods for criminal justice and criminology* (Wadsworth Cengage Learning, Belmont, CA, 2011)

E.F. McGarrell, J.D. Freilich, S. Chermak, Intelligence-led policing as a framework for responding to terrorism. J. Contemp. Crim. Justice **23**(2), 142–158 (2007)

R. McKetin, R. Sutherland, D.A. Bright, M.M. Norberg, A systematic review of methamphetamine precursor regulations. Addiction **106**(11), 1911–1924 (2011)

R.M. Medina, Social network analysis: a case study of the Islamist terrorist network. Security J. **27**(1), 97–121 (2014)

J.F. Morris, R.F. Deckro, SNA data difficulties with dark networks. Behav. Sci. Terrorism Polit. Aggression **5**(2), 70–93 (2013)

C. Morselli, Assessing vulnerable and strategic positions in a criminal network. J. Contemp. Crim. Justice **26**(4), 382–392 (2010)

C. Morselli (ed.), *Crime and networks* (Routledge, New York, 2014)

C. Morselli, K. Petit, Law-enforcement disruption of a drug importation network. Global Crime **8**(2), 109–130 (2007)

T. Mullane, *NSW Police Force crime prevention strategy 2015–2017* (New South Wales Police Force, 2015). http://www.police.nsw.gov.au/__data/assets/pdf_file/0019/392131/Crime_Prevention_Strategy_2015-2017_Online.pdf. Accessed 20 September 2016

S. Mullins, Social network analysis and counter-terrorism: measures of centrality as an investigative tool. Behav. Sci. Terrorism Polit. Aggression **5**(2), 115–136 (2012a)

S. Mullins, Social network analysis and terrorism: an introduction to the special issue. Behav. Sci. Terrorism Polit. Aggression **5**(2), 1–3 (2012b)

K. Murray, A square go: tackling organised crime where it doesn't want to be tackled. J. Money Laundering Control **16**(2), 99–108 (2013)

NCIS, *The National Intelligence Model* (NCIS, 2000). http://www.intelligence-analysis.net/National%20Intelligence%20Model.pdf. Accessed 12 July 2012

NSWPF, *New South Wales Police Force annual report 2018–2019* (2019)

A.V. Papachristos, The network structure of crime. *Sociol.* Compass **8**(4), 347–357 (2014)

S.W. Phillips, The attitudes of police managers toward intelligence-led policing. FBI Law Enforcement Bull. **81**(9), 13–17 (2012)

M. Phythian, Introduction: beyond the intelligence cycle? in *Understanding the intelligence cycle*, ed. by M. Phythian, (Taylor and Francis, Florence, 2013a)

M. Phythian (ed.), *Understanding the intelligence cycle* (Taylor and Francis, Florence, 2013b)

J. Ratcliffe, The effectiveness of police intelligence management: a New Zealand case study. Police Pract. Res. **6**(5), 435–451 (2005)

J. Ratcliffe, *Intelligence-led policing* (Routledge, New York, 2016)

J. Ritchie, J. Lewis (eds.), *Qualitative research practice: a guide for social science students and researchers* (SAGE Publications, London, 2003)

C. Rogers, The POP decade: an analysis of the problem-oriented policing approach. Police J. **83**(4), 295–303 (2010)

J. Saldana, *Fundamentals of qualitative research* (Oxford University Press, New York, 2011)

C.B. Sanders, C. Weston, N. Schott, Police innovations, 'secret squirrels' and accountability: empirically studying intelligence-led policing in Canada. Br. J. Criminol. **55**(4), 711–729 (2015)

D.M. Schwartz, T. Rouselle, Using social network analysis to target criminal networks. Trends. Org. Crime **12**(2), 188–207 (2009)

J. Sheptycki, Organizational pathologies in police intelligence systems: some contributions to the lexicon of intelligence-led policing. Eur. J. Criminol. **1**(3), 307–332 (2004)

J. Sheptycki, To go beyond the cycle of intelligence-led policing, in *Understanding the intelligence cycle*, ed. by M. Phythian, (Taylor and Francis, Florence, 2013), pp. 99–118

W.G. Skogan, The promise of community policing, in *Police innovation: contrasting perspectives*, ed. by D. Weisburd, A. A. Braga, (Cambridge University Press, Chicago, 2006), pp. 27–43

M.K. Sparrow, The application of network analysis to criminal intelligence: an assessment of the prospects. Soc. Networks **13**(3), 251–274 (1991)

I.P. Stainer, *Contemporary organisational pathologies in police information sharing: new contributions to Sheptycki's lexicon of intelligence-led policing*, Doctor of Philosophy thesis, London Metropolitan University, 2013

B. Taylor, A. Kowalyk, R. Boba, The integration of crime analysis into law enforcement agencies: an exploratory study into the perceptions of crime analysts. Police Q. **10**(154), 154–169 (2007)

R.B. Taylor, Incivilities reduction policing, zero tolerance, and the retreat from coproduction: weak foundations and strong pressures, in *Police innovation: contrasting perspectives*, ed. by D. Weisburd, A. A. Braga, (Cambridge University Press, Chicago, 2006), pp. 98–116

R.W. Taylor, E.J. Fritsch, J. Liederbach, *Digital crime and digital terrorism* (Prentice Hall Press, New Jersey, 2014)

S.J. Taylor, R. Bogdan, M. DeVault, *Introduction to qualitative research methods: a guidebook and resource* (John Wiley & Sons, Hoboken, NJ, 2016)

E.G. Van Brunsuhot, Community policing and "john schools". Can. Rev. Sociol. Anthropol. **40**(2), 215–232 (2003)

R. van der Hulst, Introduction to social network analysis (SNA) as an investigative tool. Trends. Org. Crime **12**(2), 101–121 (2009)

Victoria Police, *Victoria Police blue paper: a vision for Victoria Police 2025* (Victoria Police, 2014). http://www.police.vic.gov.au/content.asp?Document_ID=42063. Accessed 14 December 2016

Victoria Police (ed.), *Annual report 2018–2019* (Victoria Police, 2019)

G.F. Vito, J.C. Reed, W.F. Walsh, Police executives' and managers' perspectives on Compstat. Police Pract. Res. **18**(1), 15–25 (2017)

P.F. Walsh, The future of intelligence: fusion or fragmentation? J. AIPIO **19**(1), 59–90 (2011)

M. Warner, *The past and future of the intelligence cycle* (Taylor and Francis, Florence, 2013)

S. Wasserman, K. Faust, *Social network analysis: methods and applications* (Cambridge University Press, New York, 1994)

C. Whelan, *Networks and national security: dynamics, effectiveness and organisation* (Ashgate, London, 2012)

C. Whelan, B. Dupont, *Taking stock of networks across the security field: a review, typology and research agenda* (Policing and Society, 2017). http://www.tandfonline.com/doi/abs/10.1080/10439463.2017.1356297?journalCode=gpas20. Accessed 14 August 2017

C. Whelan, A. Molnar, *Policing political mega-events through 'hard' and 'soft' tactics: reflections on local and organisational tensions in public order policing* (Policing and Society, 2017). http://www.tandfonline.com/doi/full/10.1080/10439463.2017.1282481. Accessed 8 June 2017

J. Xu, H. Chen, Criminal network analysis and visualization. Commun. ACM **48**(6), 100–107 (2005)

J. Yuan, J. Cao, B. Xia, Arresting strategy based on dynamic criminal networks changing over time. Discrete Dyn. Nature Soc. **2013**, 1–9 (2013)

Social Network Analysis in the Field of Crime Intelligence: Historical Development, Application and Limitations

Introduction

The concept of a 'network', both as an organisational form and as a methodology for understanding social systems, has a long history (Borgatti et al. 2013; Whelan 2012). However, its application to criminal networks is a relatively recent development (Sparrow 1991). Network analysis concepts, in particular social network analysis (SNA), have been widely adopted by academics (Morselli 2014), leading to an extensive body of literature that explores the utility of applying SNA to criminal networks. The objective of this chapter is to review this literature with a focus on the application of SNA as an investigative tool for crime intelligence and on identifying current gaps in our understanding.

The chapter is divided into five sections. The first section briefly examines the historical development of SNA by outlining the key theories that underpin its application. The second presents Klerks' (1999) three 'generations' of network analysis as a way of understanding its development in law enforcement. The third explores the large body of literature that has applied SNA to a wide variety of criminal networks (including both terrorist and 'traditional' ones), as well as several emerging areas of

© The Author(s) 2020
M. Burcher, *Social Network Analysis and Law Enforcement*, Crime Prevention and Security Management, https://doi.org/10.1007/978-3-030-47771-4_2

application, such as cybercrime and crime prevention. This section will focus on how SNA has been applied and what it can tell us about criminal networks. The fourth section provides an in-depth examination of the challenges and limitations of applying SNA, including the size of criminal network databases, numerous data challenges and the fact that social networks are not static but constantly changing. In the final section, attention turns to the primary gaps within the SNA and law enforcement literature.

The Theory of Social Network Analysis

As SNA is both a methodology and a set of underlying theories (Papachristos 2014), it is important to understand its developmental history as it correlates with what we know about how it has been used, and in particular its capacity to contribute to one of the primary objectives of ILP, the 'disruption' of criminal networks. Borgatti et al. (2009) suggested that SNA, and network analysis more broadly, has a very long developmental history. It was not until the 1930s, however, that researchers started to put together what Freeman (2011) referred to as the four 'defining properties' of network analysis. The first property refers to the belief that social relationships between actors are important. The second states that network analysis consists of collecting and analysing data containing information relating to the relationships between actors. The third outlines the importance of displaying these relationships using graphic imagery. The fourth property highlights the need for mathematical and computational models to be used to explain the patterns of connection between actors. Freeman (2011) suggested that the first to start pulling these properties together were Jacob Moreno and Helen Jennings, who referred to their approach as 'sociometry'. In 1932 Moreno and Jennings mapped the social network of the girls attending a Hudson school in New York City (Borgatti et al. 2009). The network data consisted of the feelings each student had towards each other. Moreno and Jennings attempted to explain why in a short space of time there was a rapid increase in the number of girls running away from the school. They argued that the social network at the school allowed for the flow of social influence and ideas between the students, and that the position of each girl in that social network had a greater influence on those who ran away as opposed to other factors such as individual personalities and motivations (Borgatti et al. 2009). This type of analysis marked a critical change whereby the focus shifted from the characteristics of individuals to the *relationships* between actors (Freeman 2011).

The development of the network perspective continued during the 1950s by Pool and Kochen (1978),[1] who discussed the relationships between pairs of actors and speculated that within the US any two individuals were connected by no more than seven other actors. This article referred to what is now commonly known as the 'small world' problem (Watts and Strogatz 1998). As Borgatti et al. (2009, p. 892) explained, the small world problem is a question of 'if two persons are selected at random from a population, what are the chances that they would know each other, and, more generally, how long a chain of acquaintanceship would be required to link them?' This concept went on to influence numerous studies including the 'small world experiment' conducted by Stanley Milgram. Essentially, Milgram (1967) set out to conduct a real-world experiment of Pool and Kochen's (1978) mathematical model. Milgram wanted to know how many intermediary acquaintances would be required to connect any two people in the world. Volunteer participants were provided a folder and asked to get it to a specific target individual in another city in the US. If the participant did not know the target individual, they had to pass the folder onto someone else that they thought might know. This process would continue through as many intermediary acquaintances as necessary for the folder to reach the target individual. Milgram (1967) found on average the folder had to pass through five intermediaries, leading to the famous phrase 'six degrees of separation' (Freeman 2011). Network analysis was developed further by Mark Granovetter's (1973) seminal article, 'The strength of weak ties'. Granovetter argued that when seeking employment, one's 'weak ties', such as acquaintances, are far more important than one's 'strong ties', such as family and close friends. The basis for this argument, according to

---

[1] This article circulated for many years but was not officially published until 1978 (Freeman 2011).

Granovetter, is that an open social network (one with many acquaintances) will have access to more diverse information compared with a relatively closed network consisting of just family and close friends.

Drawing on Granovetter's theory, Ronald Burt (1992) developed the concept of 'structural holes'. A structural hole refers to the absence of a relationship between actors; for example, two groups or clusters of actors that have zero connections between them. Structural holes have been found to be of critical importance to social networks as these holes are often filled by what is referred to as a 'broker'; an actor that connects otherwise disconnected individuals or groups. Duncan J. Watts and Steven H. Strogatz (1998) continued the development of network analysis by suggesting that both natural and man-made networks consist of a central cluster, yet are still far-reaching. For example, a random individual's social network will likely consist of a number of common elements, including friends with similar backgrounds and interests. Despite there being this central cluster, these individuals are still able to connect with other actors well outside this inner group, as demonstrated by the work of Stanley Milgram.

Being able to identify and disrupt relationships, particularly those who hold brokerage positions, would have obvious benefits to law enforcement agencies that have adopted intelligence-led policing (Ratcliffe 2016). However, as Papachristos (2011, p. 101) noted, criminologists have largely 'missed the boat' when it comes to SNA. Papachristos (2011) suggested that by failing to utilise SNA, criminologists are missing an opportunity test and expand on many of the aforementioned theories as they pertain to criminal networks. That being said, Papachristos (2011) noted that since 2005, there has been a gradual uptake with criminologists using SNA. This study contributes to our understanding of SNA by examining its application, both its theoretical and methodological components, within operational law enforcement environments. While it is one question to know how criminologists are using SNA in theory, it is quite another question as to how SNA can be used in practice, particularly by law enforcement agencies.

The Development of Social Network Analysis in Law Enforcement

The 'mapping' of criminal networks has a long history within law enforcement (Harper and Harris 1975). However, the way in which law enforcement maps criminal networks has changed considerably over the years. According to Klerks (1999), the development of network analysis as an intelligence tool can be categorised into three generations. The first generation of network analysis methods consists of basic Anacapa Charts or link diagrams, and has increasingly been used in law enforcement since the mid-1970s (Calderoni 2014). This type of analysis is completed in six stages (Harper and Harris 1975). Firstly, all available information on suspected criminals, organisations and their activities is assembled. Secondly, all 'relational data' from this information, such as evidence that a meeting or phone call took place between two individuals, is extracted. Subsequently, an association matrix (also referred to as an adjacency matrix) is constructed, which consists of listing all known or targeted individuals along both the X and Y axis of a triangular graph. A simple example of an association matrix is shown in Fig. 1.

	Actor A	Actor B	Actor C	Actor D	Actor E	Actor F
Actor A						
Actor B	1					
Actor C	0	1				
Actor D	1	0	1			
Actor E	1	1	0	1		
Actor F	0	1	0	1	0	

Fig. 1 Example association matrix

Once the matrix is constructed, analysts can then easily plot whether a relationship exists (1) or not (0) between any two actors. Alternatively, a link or attribute weighting (also called interactional criteria) can be applied. These weightings can be based on different criteria, such as the 'frequency' or 'substance' of the relationships (Koschade 2006, p. 564). For example, instead of using a 1 or 0, analysts would use an arbitrary scale, such as 1–5, where 5 indicates a strong relationship and 1 a weak relationship. The choice of link or attribute weighting, and its use in general, is largely determined by the data that is available. It is more common for studies to use basic binary relationships whereby the researcher is simply addressing the question of 'does a connection exist between actor A and actor B?' (Ball 2016; Burcher and Whelan 2015; Mullins 2012; Stollenwerk et al. 2016). The use of link and attribute weightings are explored further in Chap. 4. In the fourth stage, an initial link diagram is developed. A link diagram consists of a visual representation of the association matrix whereby actors are represented by circles and their relationships are illustrated by lines running from circle to circle. Then, organisational details are added to the link diagram by drawing rectangular boxes around individuals who are known to be a part of the same sub-group. This is an effective way of identifying the individuals that connect any two groups. Lastly, the link diagram is refined, if required. This may involve moving individuals around so there are not too many overlapping lines. According to Harper and Harris (1975, p. 158), this generation of network analysis has several advantages within law enforcement, including that it can be 'easily taught to individuals who do not have a technical background; it is systematic in its application; and it produces an easily assimilated, graphic portrayal of complex relationships'. Furthermore, it can allow analysts to identify possible vulnerabilities in a network, important individuals or 'key actors', and in general, patterns of interest (Basuchowdhuri 2009; Harper and Harris 1975). However, it is a manual process that can be extremely time-consuming, a factor that suggests that applying this process to large networks would prove difficult.[2]

---

[2] For an example of how time-consuming this process can be, see Harper and Harris (1975).

The second generation of network analysis, or link analysis, is a computerised and partially automated version of the first generation. Various software, such as Analyst Notebook,[3] have been developed to allow for an association matrix to be entered and for a link diagram of the network to be automatically created. The second generation of network analysis essentially automates steps 4–6 of the first generation. Therefore, its biggest advantage is the time it saves an analyst from having to manually draw a link diagram. Another advantage is the amount of information that can be presented, as the software is capable of displaying thousands of actors and their relationships almost instantly.

There are, however, several limitations with the second generation of network analysis. The first is that the collection and collation of relational data (stages 1–3 of the first generation) remains a very labour-intensive and time-consuming process that must occur before network analysis software can be used to produce a link diagram. The second is that there is no in-depth analysis of a network's structure (Kriegler 2014; Wiil 2013). This limits the ability to interpret the position of individual actors relative to those around them and the network's overall structure. Any attempts to understand a network's structure must be undertaken manually, via a process which essentially involves looking at the link diagram and attempting to identify important actors, points of interest and possible points of vulnerability. However, previous research has shown that people tend to directly correlate an individual's physical position in a link diagram with their actual position within that network (McGrath et al. 1997; McGrath et al. 2003). For example, if an individual happens to be positioned at the top or centre of a link diagram they are likely to be considered more important than those at the bottom, regardless of that individual's actual status or position in the network. The second generation of network analysis greatly improved on the first by massively reducing the time required to produce a link diagram of a network. However, its inability to examine objectively the structure of a network means that its utility as an investigative tool is somewhat limited. The impact of this

---

[3] Analyst Notebook is a particularly popular piece of software within Australian law enforcement and overseas agencies (Cockbain et al. 2011; Marshall et al. 2008). It is used by both agencies involved in this study, Victoria Police and New South Wales Police Force.

is that many law enforcement intelligence analysts 'still use mapping software as simply a different way of presenting that which they already know, and gain little deeper knowledge about the structural forms, context and significance of the network being mapped' (Kriegler 2014, p. 2). When Klerks (1999, p. 62) outlined the three generations of network analysis, the third generation was not fully developed, but was instead in the process of being formed into 'an established methodology that [could] be taught and applied uniformly'. He envisaged that the third generation of network analysis would allow analysts to identify positions of power and influence, as well as provide a clearer understanding of the content of a network's relationships. The most important development in the evolution of network analysis has been the addition of mathematical computations to link diagrams. The combination of such computations and a link diagram is more commonly referred to as SNA. This is regarded as the 'scientific equivalent of link analysis' as it empirically and objectively examines a network's social structure (van der Hulst 2009, p. 103), thus helping to avoid personal bias among those conducting the analysis (Berlusconi 2013).[4] This is achieved by applying a wide variety of mathematical computations.[5] The following are three examples of the mathematical computations that can be applied to criminal networks, with degree centrality and betweenness centrality being particularly popular amongst researchers (Burcher and Whelan 2015; Décary-Hétu and Dupont 2012; Medina 2014; Morselli et al. 2007):

- *Degree centrality*—a measure of 'centrality' (an actor's position in a network), which is determined by the number of connections that an actor has (Borgatti et al. 2013). Someone with a high degree centrality score would be connected to a relatively large portion of a network, indicating a level of importance.

---

[4] Personal bias, also referred to as cognitive bias, can enter an analysis when a detective or analyst has preconceived notions about an actor and/or their relationships. However, it should be noted that the findings of SNA are not entirely immune to personal biases. The findings can still be influenced by the choice of which actors and relationships to include, as well as what data to incorporate in the analysis (Cockbain et al. 2011). The inclusion of mathematical computations simply helps to remove some of the bias that can enter previous generations of network analysis.

[5] A full list of mathematical computations would be too numerous to list here. See Bichler (2019); Borgatti et al. (2013); Carrington et al. (2005); and Wasserman and Faust (1994).

- *Betweenness centrality*—a measure of how often a particular actor is along the shortest path between two other actors (Borgatti et al. 2013). For example, someone with a very high betweenness score might be the only point of contact between two sub-groups within a network. High betweenness is generally associated with a position of power as that actor has the capacity to influence the flow of information and resources between actors and possibly entire groups.
- *Eigenvector centrality*—a measure of an actor's centrality relative to the centrality of adjacent actors (Borgatti et al. 2013). Eigenvector centrality is essentially a measure of popularity. Someone with a high eigenvector score would have relationships with other actors that are themselves well connected.

It is believed such measures can provide significant insights into the dynamics of criminal networks, particularly the identification of critical actors, which can then be targeted by law enforcement for disruption. It is because of these reported capabilities that a large body of literature has highlighted the potential of SNA to be used as an investigative tool (Azad and Gupta 2011; Bichler and Malm 2013; Bouchard and Nash 2015; Bright et al. 2012; Cockbain et al. 2011; Décary-Hétu and Dupont 2012; Holt 2013; Johnson and Reitzal 2011; Morselli 2010; Natarajan 2006; Rodriguez 2005; Yip 2011).

The Application of Social Network Analysis to Criminal Networks

Although the use of network analysis has been steadily growing in other fields for some time, including physics and sociology (Borgatti et al. 2009), one of the first to propose a collaboration between network theorists and intelligence analysis was Malcom Sparrow (1991). Sparrow (1991) argued that the methods and techniques inherent in network analysis would be highly applicable to intelligence analysis and that both fields would benefit from greater collaboration. For network theorists, it would result in exposure to new challenges, 'real-world' applications and new databases, while for intelligence analysts network analysis would offer the possibility of a new analytical tool (Sparrow 1991, p. 253). Despite Sparrow's (1991) ground-breaking article, the application of network theory to intelligence analysis went largely unnoticed for a decade. Following the events of 11 September 2001, however, there has been an increased interest in the capacity of SNA to better inform our understanding of criminal networks.

In one of the most influential studies in this area, Krebs (2002) mapped a portion of the network responsible for the 11 September 2001 terrorist attacks. Using open source information, including major newspapers, Krebs visually mapped and analysed the network using a variety of mathematical computations. Krebs (2002) identifies a disperse network with the 19 hijackers broken up into 4–5 actor clusters, each containing 1 pilot. The pilots were usually the only ones that connected with the other clusters. Such a dispersed network is designed to improve the group's overall security, for if any one member (other than a pilot) had been caught by law enforcement or security agencies it may have led to the capture of their own cluster, but the rest of the network would have been relatively secure from detection. Criminal and terrorist organisations based on this type of network structure have also been found to be highly adaptable (Arquilla and Ronfeldt 2002; Bakker et al. 2012; Carley 2006a; Duijn et al. 2014; Harris-Hogan 2012; Milward and Raab 2006). This was found in Kreb's examination of the 11 September group, whereby several members of the network temporarily added six connections (actors that otherwise had no relationship to one another formed new connections) in order to allow for more efficient communication and coordination in the network for a short period of time. Once the necessary planning and coordination was completed, communication between these newly formed relationships ended and the group returned to its original network structure.

Following Kreb's research, numerous studies have mapped terrorist networks to explore the potential of SNA as an investigative tool for both general and specific networks. At the general level, several studies have sought to map terrorist networks that have a global presence (see Medina 2014; Qin et al. 2005; Sageman 2004; Stollenwerk et al. 2016). For example, Qin et al. (2005, p. 287) map a large portion of the 'Global

Salafi Jihad' based on the examination of biographical data of 366 actors. One of the main findings was the ability of SNA to identify key members of the network, as those identified correlated with those considered to be important by 'domain experts' (Qin et al. 2005, p. 294). Alternatively, a number of studies have examined networks responsible for specific terrorist attacks, including the 12 October 2002 Bali bombings (Koschade 2006), the 11 March 2004 Madrid bombings (Rodriguez 2005), the 7 July and 21 July 2005 bombings/attempted bombings of the London transport system (Burcher and Whelan 2015), and the 26 November 2008 Mumbai attacks (Azad and Gupta 2011). A common finding of these studies was the identification of disperse networks with a number of dormant or weak relationships—similar properties to those that Krebs (2002) identified among the group responsible for the 9/11 attacks. These studies reinforce the concept of 'netwar' developed by Arquilla and Ronfeldt (2001), whereby terrorist groups consist not of a hierarchical structure, but a loose network form of organisation with a high degree of weak relationships. Such a concept has had a profound impact on the way we tend to think about crime and security problems, and organise in response to those (Dupont 2015; Whelan 2012).

Following Coles' (2001) critique of criminologists failure to apply SNA to what might be described as 'traditional' criminal networks (such as those involved in the manufacture and distribution of illicit drugs), there has been a much greater focus on such groups over the last five to ten years (Bouchard and Amirault 2013; Bright and Delaney 2013; Bright et al. 2015a; Bright et al. 2012; Giommoni et al. 2016). One of the leading network analysts, Carlo Morselli, has used SNA to examine criminal organisations in a variety of ways (Morselli 2009, 2010; Morselli and Giguere 2006; Morselli et al. 2007; Morselli and Petit 2007; Morselli and Roy 2008). For example, Morselli and his colleagues examined the 'security/efficiency trade-off' in criminal networks (Morselli et al. 2007, p. 143). Generally, a network with a high proportion of relationships relative to the number of actors in the network will be considered 'efficient' as information and resources can easily flow. Alternatively, a network with few relationships will theoretically be less likely to be exposed (e.g., arrested by police) and therefore is considered to be a security-oriented network. Morselli et al. (2007) compared the 11 September network examined by Krebs (2002) and a drug importation network examined by Morselli and Giguere (2006). They reaffirm Krebs' findings that the 11 September attackers constituted a disperse network with relatively few relationships (a focus on security over efficiency), and present the overall structure of the drug importation network as one with a highly connected central core with a number of peripheral actors (focus on efficiency). Overall there appears to be a clear structural difference between the two networks, which is the result of what Morselli, Giguere and Petit (2007, p. 143) referred to as 'time-to-task', meaning the interaction between time and action. Broadly speaking, Morselli et al. (2007) suggested that the time-to-task is shorter in criminal networks as they are driven by monetary gains and therefore participants will expect a 'pay-off' for their involvement in a relatively shorter amount of time compared to ideological/political networks. As a result, a certain level of efficiency (more relationships) must be maintained. On the other hand, terrorist networks, which are ideologically driven, have a much longer time-to-task as they are in action less often. According to these findings, terrorist networks are more likely to have a greater focus on security compared with traditional criminal organisations. However, this is not a universal finding. For example, the terrorist network responsible for the 2002 Bali bombings consisted of a large number of relationships relative to the number of actors involved, suggesting a high degree of efficiency (Koschade 2006). Nevertheless, the authors suggest that understanding the differences between such groups will assist law enforcement agencies in tailoring their strategies.

A further study by Morselli (2010) assessed vulnerable and strategic positions in a large illicit drug network involving the Quebec Hells Angels and their associates. Morselli (2010) aimed to distinguish between those who were in vulnerable and/or strategic positions by applying two mathematical computations, degree centrality and betweenness centrality. It was found that while a few actors had relatively high scores for both measures of centrality, the vast majority tended to favour one or the other. Morselli compared these findings with data concerning those who had actually been arrested. Not surprisingly, those with high degree centrality (associated with high 'visibility') and low betweenness centrality were far more likely to be arrested compared to those with low degree centrality and high betweenness centrality (associated with an ability to control the flow of information and/or resources in a network). This would indicate that high degree centrality is an indication of vulnerability, while betweenness centrality an indication of a form of strategic positioning. Building on this research Malm and Bichler (2011) examined the structure of the individual components that make up an illicit drug commodity chain (production and smuggling, transport, supply/distribution, and retail), believing that greater understanding in this area would assist law enforcement agencies to develop more effective strategies to combat such groups. Applying SNA to a drug commodity chain, Malm and Bichler (2011) found significant structural differences between the individual components indicating different levels of vulnerability to law enforcement disruption. For example, individuals involved in transport and supply tended to place themselves in 'brokerage' or 'bridging' positions, and thus had influence over the supply of drugs through the chain. In a similar study, Bright et al. (2015a) suggested that law enforcement agencies not only target individuals that are in strategic positions (e.g., brokerage positions) but also individuals who have access to important resources. However, as indicated in the work by Morselli (2010), those in brokerage positions tend to be less 'visible' to the attention of law enforcement agencies, suggesting that it may be better, or at least easier, for the police to target other components of the commodity chain. The study by Malm and Bichler (2011) also supports other research that found criminal organisations are not highly structured but are instead a group of loosely formed actors, often created on a case-by-case basis to achieve a particular goal (Hutchins and Benham-Hutchins 2010; Natarajan 2006).

While researchers have placed a heavy focus on the application of SNA to illicit drug networks (Bright and Delaney 2013; Bright et al. 2015a; Bright et al. 2012; Giommoni et al. 2016), SNA has also been increasingly applied to a wide variety of criminal networks engaged in other offences. For example, SNA has been applied to networks involved in the illicit art trade (Bichler et al. 2013); money laundering (Colladon and Remondi 2017; Malm and Bichler 2013; Soudijn 2014); violent crime (Bastomski et al. 2017; Bichler et al. 2016; Papachristos 2009; Papachristos et al. 2015a, b); police corruption (Lauchs et al. 2011); youth gangs and delinquent offenders (Bichler et al. 2014; Bouchard and Konaraski

2014); street gangs (McGloin 2005); fraud (Malm et al. 2014; Nash et al. 2013), and gun trafficking (Leuprecht and Aulthouse 2014). A common theme of this literature is that SNA has the capacity to provide significant insight into the structural properties of these networks and, in doing so, contribute substantially to our understanding of network *modus operandi*, as well as possible points of disruption.

There has also been research exploring several new areas of application, including cybercrime (Décary-Hétu 2014; Décary-Hétu and Dupont 2012, 2013; Holt 2013; Joffres and Bouchard 2015; Macdonald and Frank 2016; Saidi et al. 2017; Westlake et al. 2011; Yip 2011). For example, Décary-Hétu and Dupont (2012) set out to evaluate the ability of SNA to improve the value of information on cyber-criminals, including whether SNA can identify suitable targets for disruption and subsequently actors that detectives should not waste their time on. To achieve this, Décary-Hétu and Dupont (2012) applied SNA to data collected from a large police operation on computer hackers in Canada. Specifically, the operation focused on 'botmasters' (highly skilled hackers) that control 'botnets', a network of compromised computers (which can be in the thousands and even hundreds-of-thousands) that can be deployed remotely in order to steal personal and financial information, send viruses and even attack other computers. It was found that the individuals arrested by police at the end of the operation correlated strongly with those identified as important by the network analysis, suggesting that 'experienced police officers' were more than capable of identifying targets without the need to employ SNA (Décary-Hétu and Dupont 2012, p. 172). However, there were a couple of actors that appeared at the periphery of the group who, according to the analysis, potentially played a significant role in the network. Importantly, these actors were not among those arrested, suggesting that SNA is a valuable addition to existing investigative methodologies.

As Berlusconi (2017, p. 132) noted, much of the SNA literature has focused on understanding crime and terror networks, and by extension supporting 'crime enforcement'. However, a growing body of literature has been exploring the capacity of SNA to support the design and implementation of 'crime prevention' (Berlusconi 2017; Bichler et al. 2013; Bichler and Malm 2015; Bichler et al. 2014; Bright 2017; Framis and

Regadera 2017; Randle and Bichler 2017). For example, Bright (2017) applied SNA in conjunction with crime script analysis[6] to a methamphetamine network that operated in Australia in the 1990s in order to identify a possible set of crime prevention strategies to be used on organised crime groups. Bright (2017) believed that such strategies should focus on two key areas: (1) impeding the crime commission process (such as interfering with access to resources and locations); and (2) limiting the formation and development of criminal networks. From the analysis, a number of crime prevention strategies were identified. As noted earlier, individuals who are considered to be key actors in a network tend to be those who have relatively high betweenness centrality and low degree centrality (Morselli 2010). Bright (2017) identified several actors that meet this criterion in the network under investigation, suggesting that prevention strategies should focus on preventing individuals achieving such positions. It is suggested that this could be done by interventions aimed at restricting an actor's ability to remain anonymous and increasing the need for face-to-face meetings with individuals in the network. However, as Bright (2017) and others (Bichler et al. 2013) have noted, there is a concern with prevention strategies that 'displacement' may occur, whereby offenders may simply switch to a different location or crime type. That being said, crime prevention appears to be a promising area of application for SNA.

Overall, it is clear that SNA can be applied to a wide variety of criminal networks and has proven capable of providing significant insight into such groups. It is believed that this insight can assist law enforcement agencies in the development of strategies to combat criminal networks and implement crime prevention initiatives.

---

[6] Borrowing from cognitive psychology, Cornish (1994) developed a framework for establishing the step-by-step process offenders go through in order to commit a crime (their 'crime script'). The purpose of crime script analysis is to identify the elements necessary for the successful commission of a crime, including the actors, equipment, locations and activities needed. These elements allow for the *modus operandi* of a specific crime to be clearly outlined (Chiu et al. 2011). Combining crime script analysis with SNA has become increasingly popular (see Bichler et al. 2013; Brayley et al. 2011; Bright and Delaney 2013; Bruinsma and Bernasco 2004; Duijn and Klerks 2014; Morselli and Roy 2008).

The Challenges and Limitations of Social Network Analysis as Applied to Criminal Networks

Despite the considerable promise shown by the extensive body of literature suggesting that SNA is a useful tool for crime intelligence, it is not without its challenges and limitations. While Sparrow (1991, p. 261) was the first to propose the integration of SNA with criminal intelligence, he also highlighted four potential challenges or 'characteristics of criminal networks': the size of criminal databases, difficulties with incomplete data, the 'fuzzy boundaries' of a network and the dynamic nature of social networks.[7]

The first characteristic of criminal networks refers to the *size* of criminal databases and the fact that they can be incredibly large, meaning that it may not be possible to process such datasets. At the time, there were programs, such as the NEGOPY network analysis program (Richards and Rice 1981), that claimed to be able to handle networks with upwards of 30,000 connections. However, as Sparrow (1991) points out, such programs were primarily dealing with one-dimensional relations, meaning that any analysis may not take into account the complex relationships that inevitably exist not only in criminal networks but in social networks in general.

The second characteristic is the *incompleteness* of criminal network databases. These databases are a primary source of relational data necessary for the application of SNA. Difficulties with incomplete data are not a unique problem for SNA, but an issue for all analytical techniques. However, when SNA is applied to criminal networks this issue is compounded by the fact that, unlike 'open' networks, criminals actively try to hide information about themselves (Berlusconi et al. 2016). Before examining Sparrow's (1991) remaining characteristics of criminal networks it is important to note that alongside incompleteness a number of other

---

[7] The 'characteristics of criminal networks' is a somewhat misleading title of the challenges it refers to. The characteristics of criminal network *data* would be a more accurate description. However, given how widely Sparrow (1991) is cited, this study will continue to refer to these challenges by their original title.

'data challenges' have subsequently been recognised, including incorrectness, inconsistency and data transformation.

Incorrectness refers to the fact that the relational data used in SNA, including an individual's identity and their relationships, may contain inaccuracies (Morris and Deckro 2013). While this can be caused by a number of factors, one that is unique to the examination of criminal networks is that in some instances offenders will deliberately supply misinformation (Xu and Chen 2005) and/or obscure their relationships (Medina and Hepner 2008). It has also been found that confidential informants may unknowingly supply inaccurate relational data (Killworth and Bernard 1976).[8] *Inconsistency*, as its name suggests, refers to data that is inconsistently entered and stored on criminal databases. This inconsistency is often the result of human error. For example, offenders that have had multiple contacts with law enforcement may be entered into their databases more than once (Xu and Chen 2005) and subsequently appear as multiple actors. Data entry error can potentially result either in distorted findings or, in some instances, force analysts to exclude intelligence from an analysis.[9] *Data transformation* refers to the fact that once an analyst has identified and collected the relational data they need, it will often have to be converted into a usable format. SNA requires that actors be represented as nodes and their relationships represented by ties. Criminal databases, particularly older ones, were often not designed to store data in a format that can easily be used in SNA. A final issue in relation to network data is that there is no guidance for intelligence analysts on a necessary threshold of data required before analysis should be conducted, as there are no standardised criteria for data collection (Bright

---

[8] In a series of studies, Russel Bernard and Peter Killworth examined the accuracy of individuals providing relational data about social networks (Bernard and Killworth 1977, 1979, 1982; Killworth and Bernard 1976, 1979). In their first study, they had individuals simply report who they were communicating with and rank those relationships based on frequency. Of concern for law enforcement is that individuals could only accurately identify at best one-third of the individuals that they communicate with most frequently. This is even more concerning when one considers that these participants were volunteers and had no incentive to mislead the researchers.

[9] For example, a publication by the UK Home Office providing its members with a guide on how to use SNA (Gunnell et al. 2016b) and an example case study using their criminal databases (Gunnell et al. 2016a) had to omit an intelligence log from their analysis due to data entry error. In the UK, intelligence is collated into intelligence 'logs', which contain various information including the date of recording, a brief description of the offence and the individuals involved.

et al. 2012; Morris and Deckro 2013; van der Hulst 2009). Such guidelines, however, are unlikely to be developed, as they may not adequately take into consideration the different types of data that might be utilised in each application of SNA. While in some instances there is little that can be done with regard to these data challenges, the most common recommendation is to ensure that the analysis incorporates multiple sources to try and improve the accuracy of the findings (Bright et al. 2015b; Burcher and Whelan 2015; Morris and Deckro 2013; Xu et al. 2004).

The third characteristic is the issue of *fuzzy boundaries* (also called the boundary-specification problem). Although everyone is a part of a single global macro network (Duijn and Klerks 2014), the reality is that it is currently impossible to study this network in its entirety, meaning researchers and analysts have to focus on the many meso-network clusters that make up the macro network. The problem lies in determining the boundaries of these meso-networks, which is particularly problematic with criminal networks. This is considered a difficult task, as the inclusion and exclusion of actors and their relationships have the potential to change the structure of the network as it is portrayed by an SNA. For example, Borgatti et al. (2006) examined the robustness of four commonly used centrality measures—degree centrality, betweenness centrality, closeness centrality and eigenvector centrality. The study generated networks of differing size (10, 25, 50 and 100 actors) and densities (1 per cent, 2 per cent, 5 per cent, 10 per cent, 30 per cent, 50 per cent, 70 per cent and 90 per cent). Density is simply a measure of how many of the total possible ties in a network do in fact exist (Borgatti et al. 2013). For example, a network with a density score of 75 per cent means that on average each actor is connected to 75 per cent of the other actors in the network. Four different types of boundary error were then applied to these networks: node removal (the exclusion of existing actors), node addition (the inclusion of extra actors), edge deletion (the removal of network relationships) and edge addition (the inclusion of extra relationships). Borgatti et al. (2006) found that as they applied each of the four types of error, the accuracy of the centrality measures declined linearly. It was therefore concluded that the use of centrality measures is appropriate, provided that no more than 10 per cent of a network's actors/relationships are missing from the analysis. They argue that any error exceeding this threshold progressively undermines any findings. While this gives analysts some confidence in the robustness of SNA, the problem for law enforcement is that it assumes the analyst will know how much error exists in their data, which will almost never be the case (Burcher and Whelan 2015). Furthermore, the studies that have looked at the impact of fuzzy boundaries have tended to focus on quite large networks. For example, the four networks examined by Xu and Chen (2008) varied in size (104, 360, 1349 and 3917 actors respectively), in a study similar to that conducted by Borgatti et al. (2006). The problem with this is that in a network of 360 actors, it takes the addition or removal of 36 actors before the 10 per cent threshold is surpassed and the validity of any findings begins to be questioned. In a network of just 20 actors, it takes just the addition or removal of 2 actors for this threshold to be reached (see Burcher and Whelan 2015). This is an important consideration for law enforcement as there is increasing evidence to suggest that criminal groups are operating in smaller networks and are more loosely connected (Arquilla 2014; Bright et al. 2012; Kenney 2007; Natarajan 2006). While law enforcement analysts can draw some comfort from the fact that certain mathematical computations are relatively robust to errors in the boundary of a network, they need to be aware that the likelihood of these errors increases as the size of a network decreases.

The final characteristic refers to the *dynamic* nature of social networks. This recognises that the relationships and actors that make up a network are often changing. Traditional applications of SNA seek to examine and understand the relationships between actors in a network, but only at one point in time. There has been, however, an increased effort to examine the capacity of SNA to understand a network's dynamics over a period of time (a longitudinal analysis). Rather than being regarded as an extension of SNA, some see this approach as distinct and refer to it as Dynamic Network Analysis (DNA; Bichler and Malm 2013; Carley 2006b; Carley et al. 2007; Hutchins and Benham-Hutchins 2010; McCulloh and Carley 2009; Randle and Bichler 2017). Examples of dynamic networks include the examination of the development of Islamist terrorist networks in the West (Mullins and Dolnik 2010), the topography of the Noordin Top terrorist network (Everton and Cunningham 2012), the evolution of a drug-trafficking network (Bright and Delaney 2013), co-offending networks in Chicago (Charette and Papachristos 2017), a Spanish cocaine trafficking network (Framis and Regadera 2017) and the 'radicalisation trajectory' of one 'jihadi' (Nash and Bouchard 2015, p. 61). A longitudinal analysis involves applying SNA to a network multiple times and looking for any changes that might occur (such as new relationships forming). The frequency with which SNA is applied will be determined by factors such as the data that is available and the objectives of the analyst. It is believed that examining networks in this way will provide greater insight into how networks grow and evolve over time and how they respond to internal and external changes (Bright and Delaney 2013). Unlike many of the other limitations of SNA, there is a relatively clear way to overcome the fact that social networks are often changing—provided the necessary data is available.

There are several limitations of SNA that have received less attention but still have the capacity to undermine its capabilities. One of the reported capabilities of SNA is that it can contribute to the development of disruption strategies. However, a primary concern with using SNA to assist in the decision-making process concerning disruption strategies is that much of the literature fails to note that the full impact of these strategies is largely unknown and that there are just as many 'negative' potential outcomes. One outcome is that criminal networks will recover relatively easily from disruption efforts, as was found by several studies (Harris-Hogan 2012; Tsvetovat and Carley 2003). For example, an examination of an emerging 'neojihadist cell' in Sydney, Australia in 2005 by Harris-Hogan (2012) found that the targeted removal of certain actors may result in only a temporary disruption of the network. There has been some progress made in an effort to reduce the impact of this limitation. For example, Kathleen Carley and her team at Carnegie Mellon University have developed software called DyNet, which essentially conducts 'what if?' analysis. In other words, DyNet creates computer simulations of potential changes that may occur in a network as a result of various scenarios, such as the removal of an actor (Tsvetovat and Carley 2003). In general, however, this is an area in need of much research. There is also the potential for SNA to incorrectly identify actors as important, and result in what Morris and Deckro (2013) refer to as 'organisational

Darwinism': the removal of inconsequential or 'weak' members of a network that actually strengthen the group (see also Duijn et al. 2014). It is also plausible that a terrorist network may react in an extreme way to the removal or targeting of actors in their network, such as bringing forward a planned attack. Finally, the fact that disruption strategies will often avoid formal criminal justice system processes means that it can to a certain extent bypass formal mechanisms of accountability and oversight (Ratcliffe 2016).

A further limitation of SNA is that it will reportedly provide limited insight into small networks (Mullins 2012; Perliger and Pedahzur 2011). Mullins (2012) argued that it is unlikely that SNA will provide much insight into small networks when the intelligence analyst has a good qualitative understanding of the group. Visual representations of criminal networks are likely to still be of use to investigations into small networks, but the mathematical computations used in SNA are not likely to add value (Mullins 2012). Mullins (2012) suggested the real potential of SNA as an investigative tool lies in large complex networks. However, this notion has been challenged on two fronts. Firstly, there are numerous examples where SNA has been shown capable of providing insight into 'small' networks. For example, SNA has been applied to networks consisting of 12 actors (Burcher and Whelan 2015); 9 actors and 23 actors (Leuprecht and Hall 2013); 16 actors (Varese 2013); 17 actors (Koschade 2006); and the mapping of the 9/11 terrorist network, 19 actors and 37 actors (Krebs 2002). Secondly, Perliger and Pedahzur (2011) highlight the potential limitations with the application of SNA to large networks, in particular the difficulty in obtaining the necessary data. Given the problems researchers and practitioners face in procuring the information they require, it is logical to assume that this task becomes more difficult as the size of the network under investigation increases. Confusing this issue is a lack of discussion as to what constitutes 'small' and 'large' networks. For example, a 'large' network has been described as a network with as few as 237 actors (Stollenwerk et al. 2016) and as many as 4275 actors (Mainas 2012). Comparatively, in a publication by the UK Home Office presenting an example case study of SNA, a network consisting of 137 actors is described as 'relatively large' (Gunnell et al. 2016a, p. 4). It leaves analysts with no real guidance on the size of the networks most suitable for SNA.

Although SNA greatly improves on the second generation of network analysis by utilising mathematical computations, providing a level of scientific rigour to the examination of a network's structure, it often does not take into consideration important qualitative data about a network (Klerks 1999; Mullins 2012; van der Hulst 2009). For example, while SNA can identify the 'structural' position of actors in a network, it is not able to identify their 'specific' role. A structural position refers to an individual's physical position within a network, such as a 'broker'. A specific role is a reference to the 'job title' of an actor, such as the distributor in an illicit drug network. In other words, SNA often focuses on 'social capital', as in the relationships between a set of actors, at the expense of 'human capital', or the specific attributes of individual actors—particularly less visible attributes such as knowledge and expertise (Whelan 2012). Intelligence analysts will at times be able to identify the human capital each actor brings to a network from a number of sources, including informants, criminal records and physical and electronic surveillance. Although some researchers include actor attributes into their analysis of criminal networks (Basuchowdhuri 2009; Descormiers and Morselli 2011; Kaza et al. 2007), clear guidance for researchers and intelligence analysts on how this can be done remains limited (Bright et al. 2014).

Sparrow and others (Morris and Deckro 2013; Tsvetovat and Carley 2003; Xu and Chen 2005) have provided critical insight into the strengths and weaknesses of SNA. However, too little is known about what challenges exist for analysts seeking to apply SNA in operational environments and how analysts look to address these concerns. This book seeks to address this gap in understanding.

The Gaps in Knowledge of Social Network Analysis and Law Enforcement

There are several gaps in the current SNA literature concerning its application to criminal networks. One of these, according to Kennedy and Weimann (2011, p. 201), is a lack of consideration for the underlying 'sociological organisational literature within which such network theories are rooted'. They suggested that a greater appreciation of this literature will improve our understanding of crime and terrorism, as has been shown to be the case with counter-terrorism (Whelan 2012). In an effort to go some way towards addressing this apparent imbalance, Kennedy and Weimann (2011) closely examine one of the core theories of network analysis, Granovetter's (1973) strength of weak ties. Kennedy and Weimann (2011) believe that it is generally accepted that the invasion of Afghanistan to eliminate Al-Qaeda following the 11 September 2001 attacks resulted in a decentralisation of the group. However, they suggested this decentralisation may have actually strengthened the Al-Qaeda organisation. Using the strength of weak ties theory, Kennedy and Weimann (2011) explain that Al-Qaeda is likely to have access to more diverse information, ideas and resources through an expansion of their weak ties. Their research illustrates the potential for the underlying theories of SNA to provide insight into the internal operations of criminal networks.

A further limitation of the current literature is that few studies have explored the capacity of SNA to not only provide insight into the structure of criminal networks, but also their function or purpose (Leuprecht and Hall 2013). Leuprecht and Hall (2013) hypothesised that a network's structure would correlate with the group's objectives. To test this theory, they examine three US-based Al-Shabaab[10] networks, with one recruiting new members and two raising funds to be sent to Somalia in support of the group's efforts. Using SNA, Leuprecht and Hall (2013) identified a clear structural difference between the recruitment network and the two fundraising networks. The recruitment network had an 'all-channel'

---

[10] Al-Shabaab is a Somalia-based terror network (Leuprecht and Hall 2013).

structure, where members of a group are all well connected and no one actor is clearly in a crucial position or able to heavily control the flow of information. Leuprecht and Hall (2013) believed that this is due to the relatively high level of 'trust' required to recruit members. In contrast, the two fundraising networks had 'hub' structures, where generally there is one central actor who acts as a conduit for almost all communication. Leuprecht and Hall (2013) suggested that the level of trust required for a network solely established to raise funds is comparatively low, and therefore it can afford to be relatively dispersed. Leuprecht and Hall (2013) concluded that there appears to be a correlation with the structure of a terrorist network and its purpose. Understanding the structure of criminal networks in relation to their objectives has the potential to assist law enforcement agencies in developing tailored strategies to combat the illicit activities of such groups.

However, it is the contention of this study that one of the most critical gaps in the existing SNA literature concerns the fact that we know almost nothing about its use within operational law enforcement environments. As noted in the Introduction, Mullins (2012, p. 19) suggested that in order for academics to advance our understanding of SNA, there is a need for greater understanding about how it is already being used within operational law enforcement environments. SNA can be applied to a wide variety of criminal networks and it has the potential to provide substantial insight into such groups. Yet, almost all of the studies to date involve a retrospective analysis of criminal networks, often many years after they were in operation (Everton and Cunningham 2012; Harris-Hogan 2012; Mullins and Dolnik 2010; Natarajan 2006). This is due, in large part, to security concerns, and gaining access to law enforcement agencies and their data can be extremely difficult for researchers (Bright et al. 2012; Klerks 1999; Krebs 2002; Sparrow 1991). The problem lies in the fact that it is one thing to apply SNA to a criminal network once an investigation is over; it is quite a different proposition to apply SNA to a criminal network in 'real-time'—that is, while an investigation is unfolding and new information is being regularly captured. In order to truly understand the prospects of SNA as an investigative tool for crime intelligence, we need to establish whether and how it is actually being utilised within law enforcement organisations that have adopted intelligence-led policing.

In one of the few studies that has applied SNA within an operational environment, Johnson and Reitzal (2011) worked closely with the Richmond City Police (US), a large urban metropolitan police department, to develop a clearer understanding of the antecedents of conflict between rival criminal networks. Beginning with 24 actors identified as persons of interest by a gang unit at Richmond City Police, Johnson and Reitzal (2011) used the police criminal database and snowball sampling to identify any further relationships held by these individuals. They addressed the question of what might have 'set off a rash of violence between two groups of previously friendly males' (Johnson and Reitzal 2011, p. 9). By applying mathematical computations to the network over several time periods (2007 and 2008) the authors identified a fallout between two actors as the main driver behind the increased violence between two groups. Their analysis also suggested that six individuals who were vital to the operation of the criminal networks had, at that time, completely evaded the attention of law enforcement agencies. Emphasising the utility of SNA, the authors noted that after 11 analysts from both state and federal agencies received training in how to use SNA, they reported that it helped them to solve a murder case and a series of commercial robberies.

A further study by Duijn and Klerks (2014) examined the use of SNA in conjunction with crime script analysis by a regional Dutch law enforcement agency. Applying SNA to a cannabis cultivation network, they revealed several important findings, including the ability of SNA to identify information gaps and potential informants within criminal networks. They emphasised that correctly interpreting SNA requires that its outputs be combined with qualitative data. However, Duijn and Klerks (2014, p. 156) also noted that the biggest limitations of SNA are that 'it's time consuming, static and often too little too late in the eyes of law enforcement decision makers'. Nevertheless, they concluded that SNA is a useful tool for providing law enforcement insight into the hidden structures of criminal networks.

These studies strengthen the argument that SNA is a valuable addition to the tools currently available to crime intelligence analysts. They suggest that SNA can assist with intelligence collection and in the formulation of intervention strategies. In particular, much of these studies suggest that SNA can provide insight into the overall structure of a network, identify sub-groups and the position of individual actors (including potentially leaders). In doing so, these studies argue that SNA can assist law enforcement in the development of disruption strategies—a primary objective of intelligence-led policing (Ratcliffe 2016). However, this remains a very small body of literature and further study is needed. Specifically, no study to date has examined the use of SNA from the perspective of intelligence analysts.

Conclusion

This chapter examined the rapidly increasing body of literature exploring the application of SNA to criminal networks. It highlighted several key findings, including the capacity of SNA to provide insight into the internal operations of such groups, to identify actors who are critical to the network and to identify potential targets for disruption. The chapter also examined a number of inherent challenges and limitations associated with SNA, including the size of criminal databases, various data challenges, difficulties in determining the boundaries of a network and the fact that criminal groups are not static but constantly changing. It was also highlighted that little is known about what will occur once a network is disrupted, that SNA can provide insight into both large and small networks, and that it is relatively uncommon for qualitative data to be included in an analysis. Importantly, this chapter identified several gaps in our knowledge of SNA as an investigative tool for law enforcement agencies, emphasising that little is known about how SNA is being used by law enforcement and what challenges analysts may face when looking to apply it to criminal networks, given their unique organisational environment. This book addresses this gap in understanding.

References

J. Arquilla, To build a network. *Prism* **4**(1), 22–33 (2014)

J. Arquilla, D. Ronfeldt, *Networks and netwars: the future of terror, crime, and militancy* (National Defense Research Institute, Santa Monica, 2001)

J. Arquilla, D. Ronfeldt, Network revisited: the fight for the future continues. *Low Intens. Confl. Law Enforce.* **11**(2–3), 178–189 (2002)

S. Azad, A. Gupta, A quantitative assessment on 26/11 Mumbai attack using social network analysis. *J. Terror. Res.* **2**(2), 4–14 (2011)

R.M. Bakker, J. Raab, H.B. Milward, A preliminary theory of dark network resilience. *J. Policy Anal. Manage.* **31**(1), 33–62 (2012)

L. Ball, Automating social network analysis: a power tool for counter-terrorism. *Secur. J.* **29**(2), 147–168 (2016)

S. Bastomski, N. Brazil, A.V. Papachristos, Neighborhood co-offending networks, structural embeddedness, and violent crime in Chicago, *Social Networks* (2017). http://www.sciencedirect.com/science/article/pii/S0378873316302003. Accessed 18 May 2017.

P. Basuchowdhuri, *Greedy methods for approximate graph matching with applications for social network analysis*, Master of Science in Systems Science thesis, Louisiana State University, 2009.

G. Berlusconi, Do all the pieces matter? assessing the reliability of law enforcement data sources for the network analysis of wire taps. *Glob. Crime* **14**(1), 61–81 (2013)

G. Berlusconi, Social network analysis and crime prevention, in *Crime prevention in the twenty-first century: insightful approaches for crime prevention initiatives*, ed. by B. Leclerc, E. U. Savona, (Springer International Publishing, Switzerland, 2017), pp. 129–141

G. Berlusconi, F. Calderoni, N. Parolini, M. Verani, C. Piccardi, Link prediction in criminal networks: a tool for criminal intelligence analysis. *PLoS One* **11**(4), 1–21 (2016)

H.R. Bernard, P.D. Killworth, Informant accuracy in social network data II. *Human Commun. Res.* **4**(1), 3–18 (1977)

H.R. Bernard, P.D. Killworth, Informant accuracy in social network data IV: a comparison of clique-level structure in behavioral and cognitive network data. *Soc. Netw.* **2**(3), 191–218 (1979)

H.R. Bernard, P.D. Killworth, Informant accuracy in social-network data V: an experimental attempt to predict actual communication from recall data. *Soc. Sci. Res.* **11**(1), 30–66 (1982)

G. Bichler, *Understanding criminal networks* (University of California Press, Oakland, CA, 2019)

G. Bichler, S. Bush, A. Malm, Bad actors and faulty props: unlocking legal and illicit art trade. *Glob. Crime* **14**(4), 359–385 (2013)

G. Bichler, S. Lim, E. Larin, Tactical social network analysis: using affiliation networks to aid serial homicide investigation. *Homicide Stud.* **21**(2), 133–158 (2016)

G. Bichler, A. Malm, Small arms, big guns: a dynamic model of illicit market opportunity. *Glob. Crime* **14**(2–3), 261–286 (2013)

G. Bichler, A. Malm (eds.), *Disrupting criminal networks: network analysis in crime prevention* (Lynne Rienner Publishers, Boulder, CO, 2015)

G. Bichler, A. Malm, J. Enriquez, Magnetic facilities: identifying key juvenile convergence places with social network analysis. *Crime Delinq.* **60**(7), 971–998 (2014)

S. Borgatti, M. Everett, J.C. Johnson, *Analyzing social networks* (SAGE Publications, London, 2013)

S.P. Borgatti, K.M. Carley, D. Krackhardt, On the robustness of centrality measures under conditions of imperfect data. *Soc. Netw.* **28**(2), 124–136 (2006)

S.P. Borgatti, A. Mehra, D.J. Brass, G. Labianca, Network analysis in the social sciences. *Science* **323**(5916), 892–895 (2009)

M. Bouchard, J. Amirault, Advances in research on illicit networks. *Glob. Crime* **14**(2–3), 119–122 (2013)

M. Bouchard, R. Konaraski, Assessing the core membership of a youth gang from its co-offending network, in *Crime and networks*, ed. by C. Morselli, (Routledge, New York, 2014), pp. 81–93

M. Bouchard, R. Nash, Researching terrorism and counter-terrorism through a network lens, in *Social networks, terrorism, and counter-terrorism: radical and connected*, ed. by M. Bouchard, (Routledge, New York, 2015), pp. 48–60

H. Brayley, E. Cockbain, G. Laycock, The value of crime scripting: deconstructing internal child sex trafficking. *Policing* **5**(2), 132–143 (2011)

D.A. Bright, Using social network analysis to design crime prevention strategies: a case study of methamphetamine manufacture and trafficking, in *Crime prevention in the 21st Century: insightful approaches for crime prevention initiatives*, ed. by B. LeClerc, E. U. Savona, (Springer International Publishing, Switzerland, 2017), pp. 143–164

D.A. Bright, J.J. Delaney, Evolution of a drug trafficking network: mapping changes in network structure and function across time. *Glob. Crime* **14**(2–3), 238–260 (2013)

D.A. Bright, C. Greenhill, N. Levenkova, Dismantling criminal networks: can node attributes play a role? in *Crime and networks*, ed. by C. Morselli, (Routledge, New York, 2014), pp. 148–162

D.A. Bright, C. Greenhill, M. Reynolds, A. Ritter, C. Morselli, The use of actor-level attributes and centrality measures to identify key actors: a case study of an Australian drug trafficking network. *J. Contemp. Crim. Justice* **31**(3), 262–278 (2015a)

D.A. Bright, C. Greenhill, A. Ritter, C. Morselli, Networks within networks: using multiple link types to examine network structure and identify key actors in a drug trafficking operation. *Glob. Crime* **16**(3), 1–19 (2015b)

D.A. Bright, C.E. Hughes, J. Chalmers, Illuminating dark networks: a social network analysis of an Australian drug trafficking syndicate. *Crime Law Soc. Chang.* **57**(2), 151–176 (2012)

G. Bruinsma, W. Bernasco, 'Criminal groups and transnational illegal markets. *Crime Law Soc. Chang.* **41**(1), 79–94 (2004)

M. Burcher, C. Whelan, Social network analysis and small group 'dark' networks: an analysis of the London bombers and the problem of 'fuzzy' boundaries. *Glob. Crime* **16**(2), 104–122 (2015)

R. Burt, *Structural holes: the social structure of competition* (Harvard University Press, Cambridge, 1992)

F. Calderoni, Identifying mafia bosses from meeting attendance, in *Networks and network analysis for defence and security*, Lecture Notes in Social Networks, ed. A.J. Masys (Springer, Switzerland, 2014), pp. 27–48

K.M. Carley, Destabilization of covert networks. *Comput. Math. Organ. Th.* **12**(1), 51–66 (2006a)

K.M. Carley, *A dynamic network approach to the assessment of terrorist groups and the impact of alternative courses of action*, paper presented to Visualising Network Information, Neuilly-sur-Seine, France, 2006b.

K.M. Carley, J. Diesner, J. Reminga, M. Tsvetovat, Toward an interoperable dynamic network analysis toolkit. *Decis. Support Syst.* **43**(4), 1324–1347 (2007)

P.J. Carrington, J. Scott, S. Wasserman, *Models and methods in social network analysis* (Cambridge University Press, Cambridge, 2005)

Y. Charette, A.V. Papachristos, The network dynamics of co-offending careers, *Social Networks* (2017). http://www.sciencedirect.com/science/article/pii/S0378873316302234. Accessed 25 May 2017.

Y.-N. Chiu, B. Leclerc, M. Townsley, Crime script analysis of drug manufacturing in clandestine laboratories: implications for prevention. *Br. J. Criminol.* **51**(2), 355–374 (2011)

E. Cockbain, H. Brayley, G. Laycock, Exploring internal child sex trafficking networks using social network analysis. *Policing* **5**(2), 144–157 (2011)

N. Coles, It's not what you know it's who you know: analysing serious crime groups as social networks. *Br. J. Criminol.* **41**(4), 580–594 (2001)

A.F. Colladon, E. Remondi, Using social network analysis to prevent money laundering. *Expert Syst. Appl.* **67**, 49–58 (2017)

D. Cornish, The procedural analysis of offending and its relevance for situational prevention, in *Crime prevention studies*, ed. by R. V. Clarke, (Criminal Justice Press, New York, 1994), pp. 151–196

D. Décary-Hétu, Information exchange paths in IRC hacking chat rooms, in *Crime and networks*, ed. by C. Morselli, (Routledge, New York, 2014)

D. Décary-Hétu, B. Dupont, The social network of hackers. *Glob. Crime* **13**(3), 160–175 (2012)

D. Décary-Hétu, B. Dupont, Reputation in a dark network of online criminals. *Glob. Crime* **14**(2–3), 175–196 (2013)

K. Descormiers, C. Morselli, Alliances, conflicts, and contradictions in Montreal's street gang landscape. *Int. Crim. Justice Rev.* **21**(3), 297–314 (2011)

P.A.C. Duijn, V. Kashirin, P.M.A. Sloot, The relative ineffectiveness of criminal network disruption. *Sci. Rep.* **4**(4238), 1–15 (2014)

P.A.C. Duijn, P.P.H.M. Klerks, Social network analysis applied to criminal networks: recent developments in Dutch law enforcement, in *Networks and network analysis for defence and security*, ed. by A. J. Masys, (Springer, Heidelberg, 2014), pp. 121–159

B. Dupont, Security networks and counter-terrorism: a reflection on the limits of adversarial isomorphism, in *Social networks, terrorism and counter-terrorism: radical and connected*, ed. by M. Bouchard, (Routledge, London, 2015), pp. 155–174

S.F. Everton, D. Cunningham, Detecting significant changes in dark networks. *Behav. Sci. Terrorism Polit. Aggression* **5**(2), 1–21 (2012)

A.G.-S. Framis, S.F. Regadera, Static and dynamic approaches of a drug trafficking network, in *Crime prevention in the twenty-first century: insightful approaches for crime prevention initiatives*, ed. by B. Leclerc, E. U. Savona, (Springer International Publishing, Switzerland, 2017)

L.C. Freeman, *The SAGE handbook of social network analysis*, eds. J. Scott, P.J. Carrington, SAGE Publications Ltd., 2011. https://uk.sagepub.com/en-gb/eur/the-sage-handbook-of-social-network-analysis/book232753. Accessed 14 May 2012.

L. Giommoni, A. Aziani, G. Berlusconi, How do illicit drugs move across countries? a network analysis of the heroin supply to Europe. *J. Drug Issues* **47**(2), 217–240 (2016)

M. Granovetter, The strength of weak ties. *Am. J. Sociol.* **78**(6), 1360–1380 (1973)

D. Gunnell, J. Hillier, L. Blakeborough, *Social network analysis of an urban street gang using police intelligence data* (2016a). https://www.gov.uk/government/uploads/system/uploads/attachment_data/file/491578/horr89.pdf. Accessed 22 April 2016.

D. Gunnell, J. Hillier, L. Blakeborough, *Social network analysis: how to guide* (2016b). https://www.gov.uk/government/uploads/system/uploads/attachment_data/file/491572/socnet_howto.pdf. Accessed 22 April 2016.

W.R. Harper, D.H. Harris, The application of link analysis to police intelligence. *Hum. Factors* **17**(2), 157–164 (1975)

S. Harris-Hogan, Anatomy of a terrorist cell: a study of the network uncovered in Sydney in 2005. *Behav. Sci. Terrorism Polit. Aggression* **5**(2), 1–18 (2012)

T.J. Holt, Exploring the social organisation and structure of stolen data markets. *Glob. Crime* **14**(2–3), 155–174 (2013)

C.E. Hutchins, M. Benham-Hutchins, Hiding in plain sight: criminal network analysis. *Comput. Math. Organ. Th.* **16**(1), 89–111 (2010)

K. Joffres, M. Bouchard, Vulnerabilities in online child exploitation networks, in *Disrupting criminal networks: network analysis in crime prevention*, ed. by G. Bichler, A. Malm, (Lynne Rienner Publishers, Boulder, CO, 2015), pp. 153–175

J.A. Johnson, J.D. Reitzal, *Social network analysis in an operational environment: defining the utility of a network approach for crime analysis using the Richmond City Police Department as a case study* (2011). http://www.coginta.org/en/document/policy_working_paper_series?page=3. Accessed 8 August 2012.

S. Kaza, H. Daning, C. Hsinchun, Dynamic social network analysis of a dark network: identifying significant facilitators, *Intelligence and Security Informatics, 2007 IEEE* (2007), pp. 40–6.

J. Kennedy, G. Weimann, The strength of weak terrorist ties. *Terror. Political Violence* **23**(2), 201–212 (2011)

M. Kenney, The architecture of drug trafficking: network forms of organisation in the Colombian cocaine trade. *Glob. Crime* **8**(3), 233–259 (2007)

P.D. Killworth, H.R. Bernard, Informant accuracy in social network data. *Hum. Organ.* **35**(3), 269–286 (1976)

P.D. Killworth, H.R. Bernard, Informant accuracy in social network data III: a comparison of triadic structure in behavioural and cognitive data. *Soc. Netw.* **2**(1), 19–46 (1979)

P. Klerks, The network paradigm applied to criminal organisations: theoretical nitpicking or relevant doctrine for investigators? Recent developments in the Netherlands. *Connections* **24**(3), 53–65 (1999)

S. Koschade, A social network analysis of Jemaah Islamiyah: the applications to counterterrorism and intelligence. *Stud. Confl. Terror.* **29**(6), 559–575 (2006)

V. Krebs, Mapping networks of terrorist cells. *Connections* **24**(3), 43–52 (2002)

A. Kriegler, Using social network analysis to profile organised crime. *Institute Secur. Stud.* **57**, 1–8 (2014)

M. Lauchs, R. Keast, N. Yousefpour, Corrupt police networks: uncovering hidden relationship patterns, functions and roles. *Polic. Soc.* **21**(1), 110–127 (2011)

C. Leuprecht, A. Aulthouse, Guns for hire: North America's intra-continental gun trafficking networks. *Criminol. Crimi. Justice Law Soc.* **15**(3), 57–74 (2014)

C. Leuprecht, K. Hall, Networks as strategic repertoires: functional differentiation among Al-Shabaab terror cells. *Glob. Crime* **14**(2–3), 287–310 (2013)

M. Macdonald, R. Frank, The network structure of malware development, deployment and distribution. *Glob. Crime* **18**(1), 49–69 (2016)

E.D. Mainas, The analysis of criminal and terrorist organisations as social network structures: a quasi-experimental study. *Int. J. Police Sci. Manag.* **14**(3), 264–283 (2012)

A. Malm, G. Bichler, Networks of collaborating criminals: assessing the structural vulnerability of drug markets. *J. Res. Crime Delinq.* **48**(2), 271–297 (2011)

A. Malm, G. Bichler, Using friends for money: the positional importance of money-launderers in organized crime. *Trends Org. Crime* **16**(4), 365–381 (2013)

A. Malm, A. Schoepfer, G. Bichler, N. Boyd, Pushing the Ponzi: the rise and fall of network fraud, in *Crime and Networks*, ed. by C. Morselli, (Routledge, New York, 2014), pp. 249–262

B. Marshall, H. Chen, S. Kaza, Using importance flooding to identify interesting networks of criminal activity. *J. Am. Soc. Inf. Sci. Tec.* **59**(13), 2099–2114 (2008)

I. McCulloh, K.M. Carley, *Longitudinal dynamic network analysis: using the over time viewer feature in ORA*, Carnegie Mellon University, 2009. https://papers.ssrn.com/sol3/papers.cfm?abstract_id=2729276. Accessed 14 April 2015.

J.M. McGloin, Policy and intervention considerations of a network analysis of street gangs. *Criminol. Public Policy* **4**(3), 607–635 (2005)

C. McGrath, J. Blythe, D. Krackhardt, The effect of spatial arrangement on judgments and errors in interpreting graphs. *Soc. Netw.* **19**(3), 223–242 (1997)

C. McGrath, D. Krackhardt, J. Blythe, Visualizing complexity in networks: seeing both the forest and the trees. *Connections* **25**(1), 37–47 (2003)

R. Medina, G. Hepner, Geospatial analysis of dynamic terrorist networks, in *Values and violence: intangible aspects of terrorism*, ed. by I. A. Karawan, W. McCormack, S. E. Reynolds, (Springer, Dordrecht, 2008), pp. 151–167

R.M. Medina, Social network analysis: a case study of the Islamist terrorist network. *Secur. J.* **27**(1), 97–121 (2014)

S. Milgram, The small-world problem. *Psychol. Today* **1**(1), 61–67 (1967)

H. Milward, J. Raab, Dark networks as organizational problems: elements of a theory. *Int. Public Manag. J.* **9**(3), 333–360 (2006)

J.F. Morris, R.F. Deckro, SNA data difficulties with dark networks. *Behav. Sci. Terrorism Polit. Aggression* **5**(2), 70–93 (2013)

C. Morselli, Hells Angels in springtime. *Trends Org. Crime* **12**(2), 145–158 (2009)

C. Morselli, Assessing vulnerable and strategic positions in a criminal network. *J. Contemp. Crim. Justice* **26**(4), 382–392 (2010)

C. Morselli (ed.), *Crime and networks* (Routledge, New York, 2014)

C. Morselli, C. Giguere, Legitimate strengths in criminal networks. *Crime Law Soc. Chang.* **45**(3), 185–200 (2006)

C. Morselli, C. Giguere, K. Petit, The efficiency/security trade-off in criminal networks. *Soc. Netw.* **29**(1), 143–153 (2007)

C. Morselli, K. Petit, Law-enforcement disruption of a drug importation network. *Glob. Crime* **8**(2), 109–130 (2007)

C. Morselli, J. Roy, Brokerage qualifications in ringing operations. *Criminol.* **46**(1), 71–98 (2008)

S. Mullins, Social network analysis and counter-terrorism: measures of centrality as an investigative tool. *Behav. Sci. Terrorism Polit. Aggression* **5**(2), 115–136 (2012)

S. Mullins, A. Dolnik, An exploratory, dynamic application of social network analysis for modelling the development of Islamist terror cells in the West. *Behav. Sci. Terrorism Polit. Aggression* **2**(1), 3–29 (2010)

R. Nash, M. Bouchard, Travel broadens the network: turning points in the trajectory of an American jihadi, in *Social networks, terrorism, and counter-terrorism: radical and connected*, ed. by M. Bouchard, (Routledge, New York, 2015), pp. 61–81

R. Nash, M. Bouchard, A. Malm, Investing in people: the role of social networks in the diffusion of a large-scale fraud. *Soc. Netw.* **35**(4), 686–698 (2013)

M. Natarajan, Understanding the structure of a large heroin distribution network: a quantitative analysis of qualitative data. *J. Quant. Criminol.* **22**(2), 171–192 (2006)

A.V. Papachristos, Murder by structure: dominance relations and the social structure of gang homicide. *Am. J. Sociol.* **115**(1), 74–128 (2009)

A.V. Papachristos, The coming of a Networked Criminology, in *Measuring crime and criminality: advances in criminological theory*, ed. J. MacDonald (Taylor and Francis, 2011), pp. 101–140

A.V. Papachristos, The network structure of crime. *Sociol. Compass* **8**(4), 347–357 (2014)

A.V. Papachristos, A.A. Braga, E. Piza, L.S. Grossman, The company you keep? the spillover effects of gang membership on individual gunshot victimization in a co-offending network. *Criminol.* **53**(4), 624–649 (2015a)

A.V. Papachristos, C. Wildeman, E. Roberto, Tragic, but not random: the social contagion of nonfatal gunshot injuries. *Soc. Sci. Med.* **125**, 139–150 (2015b)

A. Perliger, A. Pedahzur, Social network analysis in the study of terrorism and political violence. *Polit. Sci. Polit.* **44**(2), 45–50 (2011)

I.S. Pool, M. Kochen, Contacts and influence. *Soc. Netw.* **1**(1), 5–51 (1978)

J. Qin, J.J. Xu, D. Hu, M. Sageman, H. Chen, Analyzing terrorist networks: a case study of the global jihad. *Lect. Notes Comput. Sci.* **3495**, 287–304 (2005)

J. Randle, G. Bichler, Uncovering the social pecking order in gang violence, in *Crime prevention in the twenty-first century: insightful approaches for crime prevention initiatives*, ed. by B. Leclerc, E. U. Savona, (Springer International Publishing, Switzerland, 2017)

J. Ratcliffe, *Intelligence-led policing* (Routledge, New York, 2016)

W.D. Richards, R.E. Rice, The NEGOPY network analysis program. *Soc. Netw.* **3**(3), 215–223 (1981)

J.A. Rodriguez, *The March 11th terrorist network: in its weakness lies its strength*, CiteSeer (2005). http://citeseerx.ist.psu.edu/viewdoc/summary?doi= 10.1.1.98.4408. Accessed 7 August 2012.

M. Sageman, *Understanding terror networks* (University of Pennsylvania Press, Philadelphia, 2004)

F. Saidi, Z. Trabelsi, K. Salah, H.B. Ghezala, Approaches to analyze cyber terrorist communities: survey and challenges. *Comput. Secur.* **66**, 66–80 (2017)

M.R.J. Soudijn, Using strangers for money: a discussion on money-launderers in organized crime. *Trends Org. Crime* **17**(3), 199–217 (2014)

M.K. Sparrow, The application of network analysis to criminal intelligence: an assessment of the prospects. *Soc. Netw.* **13**(3), 251–274 (1991)

E. Stollenwerk, T. Dörfler, J. Schibberges, Taking a new perspective: mapping the Al Qaeda network through the eyes of the UN Security Council. *Terror. Political Violence* **28**(5), 950–970 (2016)

M. Tsvetovat, K.M. Carley, *Bouncing back: recovery mechanisms of covert networks*, paper presented to NAACSOS Conference, Pittsburgh, PA, 2003. http://www.casos.cs.cmu.edu/publications/working_papers/tsvetovat_2003_recovery.pdf.

R. van der Hulst, Introduction to social network analysis (SNA) as an investigative tool. *Trends Org. Crime* **12**(2), 101–121 (2009)

F. Varese, The structure and the content of criminal connections: the Russian mafia in Italy. *Eur. Sociol. Rev.* **29**(5), 899–909 (2013)

S. Wasserman, K. Faust, *Social network analysis: methods and applications* (Cambridge University Press, New York, 1994)

D.J. Watts, S.H. Strogatz, Collective dynamics of 'small-world' networks. *Nature* **393**(6684), 440–442 (1998)

B.G. Westlake, M. Bouchard, R. Frank, Finding the key players in online child exploitation networks. *Policy Internet* **3**(2), 1–32 (2011)

C. Whelan, *Networks and national security: Dynamics, effectiveness and organisation* (Ashgate, London, 2012)

U.K. Wiil, *Issues for the next generation of criminal network investigation tools*, paper presented to European Intelligence and Security Informatics Conference, Uppsala, Sweden, 2013.

J. Xu, H. Chen, Criminal network analysis and visualization. *Commun. ACM* **48**(6), 100–107 (2005)

J. Xu, H. Chen, The topology of dark networks. *Commun. ACM* **51**(10), 58–65 (2008)

J. Xu, B. Marshall, S. Kaza, H. Chen, Analyzing and visualizing criminal network dynamics: a case study, in *Intelligence and Security Informatics*, ed. by H. Chen, R. Moore, D. D. Zeng, J. Leavitt, vol. 3073, (Springer, Berlin/Heidelberg, 2004), pp. 359–377.

M. Yip, *An investigation into Chinese cybercrime and the applicability of social network analysis*, paper presented to ACM WebSci 11, 14–17 June 2011, Koblenz, Germany, 2011.

3

Social Network Analysis and Crime Intelligence

Introduction

This chapter will explore the role of social network analysis (SNA) within crime intelligence. As outlined in Chap. 2, despite the significant body of research that has explored the application of SNA to crime intelligence (Bouchard and Amirault 2013; Morselli 2014), very few studies have actually examined its use within operational law enforcement environments (Duijn and Klerks 2014; Johnson and Reitzal 2011). No study has examined the use of SNA by law enforcement in Australia. To truly understand the prospects of SNA as an investigative tool it is critical that we understand how it is already being used by law enforcement and the challenges arising when attempting to apply it to criminal networks. This chapter addresses the first objective of this study: to identify *whether* SNA is being used by intelligence analysts in operational law enforcement environments in Australia, and if so *how*.

The chapter is divided into two sections. The first section will establish whether interviewees are using SNA or alternative 'network analysis' methodologies. To achieve this, this section will draw on Klerks' (1999) three generations of network analysis development. The second section

© The Author(s) 2020   **65**
M. Burcher, *Social Network Analysis and Law Enforcement*, Crime Prevention and Security Management, https://doi.org/10.1007/978-3-030-47771-4_3

will focus on how the current generation of network analysis, SNA, is being used by intelligence analysts operating within intelligence-led policing (ILP). This includes using SNA to identify network vulnerabilities and further avenues of enquiry. This section also examines the use of 'link' and 'attribute' weights by analysts, and perspectives on when SNA should be applied.

Are Intelligence Analysts Using Social Network Analysis?

Law enforcement has a long history of attempting to map criminal networks (Harper and Harris 1975). As one analyst notes, 'creating a map of the crime environment is one of the most important things [we do] and that's where that whole idea of understanding the social network actually stands up and is a very strong tool' (Analyst No. 19). However, under the umbrella term 'network analysis' there is a wide variety of analytical tools of which SNA is just one. While SNA has received extensive attention by researchers, it is largely unknown if it is being used by law enforcement or if alternative network approaches are preferred (Duijn and Klerks 2014). The first generation of network analysis consists of basic hand-drawn charts showing who is connected to whom (Klerks 1999). Given that this process can be incredibly time-consuming, it was somewhat surprising to find that several analysts interviewed at times still chose to conduct this type of network analysis:

> I manually draw a lot of my organisational structure charts based on all the information that we have gleaned. And at the end of the day I find that easier to do that because I get to know the investigation, who they are, going over the data helps me recall who they are and why they are important and add little bits to that. (Analyst No. 21)

> The good old whiteboard with drawing the main players [...], it tends to give your mind a better picture [...], you can see and you can draw all the lines [...]. The picture becomes much clearer than trying to shuffle individual bits of paper around or read and put it all into your head. If you

just put it on in simple terms, it just makes so much better sense, the picture is much clearer. (Analyst No. 13)

It should be noted that these few analysts knew how to use second- and, in some cases, third-generation network analysis tools. However, they felt that when looking at groups with few actors/relationships involved, hand-drawn networks still have a place within law enforcement as they provide analysts with a relatively quick and 'better sense' of the targeted network, over individual documents or reports. That being said, because of the time-consuming nature of the first generation of analysis on a network of even moderate size (Harper and Harris 1975), and in part as a result of the increased volume of data now being collected by law enforcement agencies and available for inclusion in network analysis (see Chap. 7), it was inevitable that analysts would look for alternative approaches to meet these challenges. This had led to the overwhelming majority of interviewees moving beyond the first generation of network analysis.

The second generation of network analysis improves substantially on the first by using various software programs to partially automate the production of a link diagram (or visual representation of a network). As one analyst explained, 'when you use Analyst Notebook [...], particularly when you have large amounts of data [...], the picture is much clearer' (Analyst No. 13). When Klerks (1999, p. 54) first described the three generations of network analysis he argued that many intelligence analysts, at least within Dutch Law enforcement, had been trained to use such software programs but that their level of sophistication remained 'modest' and focused only on producing link diagrams. Two and a half decades later, it is evident from many analysts interviewed that producing a visual representation of criminal networks remains a priority:

Okay, so it's [network analysis] more of a pictorial view or presentation rather than a list or report or a story. It's more of a pictorial presentation of activity, [...] it's forming links and connections to people [...]. So, to put that in a network or to do it as a network analysis, provides you with a bigger picture or better picture. It can save you time and can give you an overall picture or overall view. It can present a vast amount of data in one group or one presentation, whereas to do that in the conventional method [first generation of network analysis] would take ages and ages, it's not possible to present that look. (Analyst No. 3)

I think the good detectives[1] use us to draw maps for them. [Because] if they're doing surveillance, if they're doing telephone intercepts, they can do it that way. But when it comes down to researching stuff, that's a little bit outside of their scope, looking at the frequency of things, what kind of patterns are showing up here, how would I get this information, sometimes they're at sea [outside their understanding]. (Analyst No. 19)

An interesting point raised by only one analyst was that they felt within their organisation there was too much of a focus on the physical layout of the actors and their relationships within a link diagram and not enough time spent *understanding* those relationships: 'we take time to do the spacing, not overlapping and everything like that [to ensure that] we've got a nice pretty chart rather than looking at the relationships' (Analyst No. 22). The concern here is that analysts will draw incorrect conclusions from these link diagrams based simply on their arbitrary layout (van der Hulst 2009). As outlined in Chap. 2, link diagrams can easily be misinterpreted (McGrath et al. 1997, 2003). For example, the close proximity of any two actors in a link diagram will often be interpreted to mean that they are from the same group. Two connected actors appearing visually close together or far apart in a link diagram has no reflection on the quality or substance of that relationship. Aside from when link and attribute weightings are used (explored later in this chapter), link diagrams simply show who is connected to whom. It was clear from the research participants that they felt this type of visual representation of a criminal network is useful. It was also evident that for a few analysts their skill set was limited to this type of second-generation network analysis. As one analyst explained when asked about SNA: 'I can honestly say I probably don't have a very good understanding at all' (Analyst No. 27). The majority of interviewees, however, had tried the third generation of network analysis, with many suggesting they use it regularly.

---

[1] Interviewees from both Victoria Police and New South Wales Police Force use the terms 'detective' and 'investigator' interchangeably.

The third generation of network analysis, or simply SNA, seeks to improve upon the second generation by introducing a degree of scientific rigour and objectivity to the analysis through the use of a wide variety of mathematical computations (van der Hulst 2009). SNA can reportedly identify the position of actors within a network, the structure of the network as a whole and in general assist law enforcement in developing strategies to combat criminal networks (Berlusconi 2013; Mainas 2012; Mullins and Dolnik 2010). This ability to assist with the development of disruption strategies, including the identification of points of vulnerability within criminal networks, was recognised by the majority of the research participants as a primary reason for using SNA:

> Social network analysis to me is understanding the relationships in a group and how people influence one another. Also, it provides police with the opportunity to perhaps, by understanding these relationships and the different influences, to manipulate that or to position our operations to certain areas where we think we will get our most valuable information or intelligence or result. (Analyst No. 22)

> Network analysis is really looking at what the size of the network is, what the different people bring to the network, the strength of their connections, the vulnerabilities that you might be able to identify in that network, where concentrating or having some sort of activity around a part of that network might either assist or impact the rest of the network. It's really getting an idea of, […] have we got the full vision of what we're trying to investigate. (Analyst No. 8)

> I would like to say that I think personally, social network analysis is getting some attention. The criminal environment is getting quite complex, especially in regards to counter-terrorism threats. So, it's quite vital we make use of any tool that we can have at our disposal to actually identify networks for disruption. (Analyst No. 16)

Another reported capability of SNA is that it can help to overcome cognitive biases (Cockbain et al. 2011), as analysts and detectives may have preconceived notions about a network (Berlusconi 2013; Bichler et al. 2016; Kebbell et al. 2010; Rossmo 2009). For example, according to Dr D. Kim Rossmo, a former detective with the Vancouver Police Department, there are a number of cognitive biases (or personal biases) that officers within law enforcement agencies are susceptible to, such as 'tunnel vision' where detectives and analysts develop a narrow focus on an individual and fail to consider alternative suspects (Rossmo 2009, pp. 13–14). The ability of SNA to help avoid cognitive biases was recognised by several analysts and was one of the reasons why they chose to use it:

> It's just a tool to overcome your own personal biases. (Analyst No. 23)

> Investigators may have a bee in their bonnet about some youth group, they're always causing trouble, and I guess the SNA could say well no they're not causing trouble. (Analyst No. 11)

It was evident from the research participants that they believed that SNA could assist law enforcement in the formulation of strategies designed to combat criminal networks and to potentially overcome their own cognitive biases or those of their colleagues. While it was clear that they saw value in SNA as an investigative tool, there was far less consensus when it came to *how* SNA should be applied.

Application of Social Network Analysis in Intelligence-Led Policing

The following sections seek to further our understanding of *how* SNA is being used within ILP. The findings from this study suggest SNA is being applied and utilised in four key ways: identifying key actors and network vulnerabilities; identifying further avenues of enquiry; by incorporating link weights into the analysis; and by conducting SNA at different stages of an investigation.

Key Actors and Network Vulnerabilities

Within the SNA literature there has been an immense focus on the capacity of SNA to identify key actors and points of vulnerability within criminal networks (Azad and Gupta 2011; Ball 2016; Bright et al. 2012, 2015b; Cockbain et al. 2011; Klerks 1999; Koschade 2006; Mac Ginty 2010; Malm and Bichler 2011; Morselli 2010). Even so, we do not know whether law enforcement agencies are using SNA in this way. Among the analysts interviewed, many use SNA to identify possible points of vulnerability within criminal networks. As several analysts explained:

> So, when you have your network and you click on social network analysis, what do you want, do you want eigenvector, degree and betweenness and closeness, and I think k-core[2] is a new one, and you go yeah, I want all those, those sound great, and you tick them all and you get these scores [...]. What I'm usually drawn to, is to go, who's the bridging person between this group of offenders and that group of offenders, because in network analysis that's a weak point. If we can cut that, any common benefits between these two groups will in theory be snipped, gone. (Analyst No. 2)

> How I've used social network analysis is the tool within Analyst Notebook [...]. I've used it with I guess larger networks, it just helps to make it clearer who are the more powerful players, that might not be obvious. You might have a whole bunch of people, you know little bits of information about them, it's a whole web and nothing stands out in particular and social network analysis and the different centralities might help you understand who might be more senior, where you might want to position certain resources, [and] where weaknesses are which is critical. [...] It should be something that we're doing with every investigation, [...] it should [also] be happening before that as a targeting tool. (Analyst No. 22)

---

[2] A k-core is 'a subgraph in which every actor has degree k or more with the other actors in the subgraph. Hence in a 2-core every actor is connected to at least two other actors' (Borgatti et al. 2013, p. 252). A k-core analysis is particularly useful for analysts who are looking at very large networks, but wish to focus on the core of the network. For example, once a k-core analysis has been conducted, the analyst can progressively remove actors who are one-core (who have a relationship with only one actor), two-core (who have a relationship with only two actors) and so on until they are left with just 'the inner core of the network' (Borgatti et al. 2013, p. 252).

This approach of identifying individuals seen as either key actors and/ or points of vulnerability fits within the objectives of ILP (Ratcliffe 2016) and the broader strategy of 'disruption' outlined in the Introduction to this book. As alluded to in the previous quote and discussed in greater detail by another analyst, a further benefit of targeting key actors is that it can help ensure resources are allocated efficiently:

> We are very resource driven and we don't have an infinite amount of resources to throw at investigations. The ability to be able to identify I guess best bang for your buck, to be able to identify if we are going to be able to target a group, where and what is going to be the most effective way to disrupt this group [...]. It may be a matter of identifying that this group is that rock solid that this isn't going to happen, but we might be able to identify what is a driver for this group and if we can identify a way of removing or eliminating that driver then that in effect may bring that group's crime activities to a grinding halt, if we are able to control that driver. So, it again provides a number of avenues in relation to targeting, identifying best resource allocation and processes, as well as potentially identifying some of the drivers and methods to potentially disrupt. (Analyst No. 17)

The ability of SNA to help guide decision-making around resource allocation during the target selection process is likely to be of benefit to agencies seeking to embrace ILP. However, as the analyst above notes, SNA might identify that some networks are 'rock solid', meaning that the targeting of certain actors is unlikely to disrupt the network. This itself is a useful finding for investigators, suggesting that when networks are found unlikely to be affected by disruption strategies targeting key actors, alternative strategies should be explored. This also reinforces the notion that SNA should not be a substitute for decision-making with regard to target selection; instead it should simply form one part of the decision-making process (Roberts and Everton 2011). This is important given that the targeting of individuals based on their structural position within a network has its limitations. For example, it was noted in Chap. 2 that loosely connected networks have proven to be resilient and capable of recovering relatively quickly from the removal of actors (Carley 2006a;

Duijn et al. 2014; Dupont 2015). It is argued that factors such as the overall structure of a network (including hierarchical, cell-based or loosely connected groups) and the early targeting of a network before it has the opportunity to organise or re-organise after already being targeted are critical factors in determining whether or not various forms of disruption will be effective (Carley 2006a; Duijn et al. 2014; Leuprecht et al. 2016). It was suggested by one analyst that the limited effectiveness of targeting certain actors for removal is in part the result of changes in the criminal environment, whereby criminal networks have adopted an 'entrepreneurial model':

> The idea of a cut point between different criminal groups, that there is one crucial relationship that crosses the boundary between different criminal gangs or groups. That if we were to remove one of those participants it would reduce the capability of those groups through no longer having access to those groups and also the concept of removing one crucial facilitator within a single group, those concepts are valuable to us and have been over the years. Our feeling is those capabilities or that approach to be able to degrade the performance of a criminal group by successfully removing one participant has reduced over time and through the phenomenon of an entrepreneurial crime model if you like, versus the old hierarchical crime model or mafia style view. The entrepreneurial model sees underlings if you like, not only waiting for a particular crucial facilitator to be removed from the picture but are opportunistically trying to develop the relationship with the partner organisation, with the other criminal group in advance of that and the value of removing any one significant person in my belief has been reduced today compared to what it might have been in the past. (Analyst No. 18)

According to this analyst, a change in the organisation of criminal networks, whereby they have gone from a hierarchical structure to adopting an 'entrepreneurial model' (characterised by loose connections and opportunistic actors), has reduced the effectiveness of targeting 'key actors' for disruption. This shift in organisational structure by criminal groups has been noted elsewhere (Décary-Hétu and Dupont 2012; Kenney 2007). For example, in an analysis of the Colombian drug trade Kenney (2007) found a number of 'narcos' had deliberately segmented their operations into small groups that had very little contact with the rest of the network. However, it should be noted that just because a network is loosely connected does not mean that there is an absence of authority or leadership (Leuprecht et al. 2016). A network can be loosely connected and can maintain a hierarchy. Nevertheless, due to the resilience of loosely connected criminal networks (Harris-Hogan 2012; Tsvetovat and Carley 2005), this would suggest that while SNA may be able to identify key actors and possible points of vulnerability in such groups, implementing disruption strategies in operational environments is extremely difficult.

A concern raised by only one analyst is that they and many of their fellow analysts have a poor understanding of the theories that underpin SNA, such as Burt's (1992) 'structural holes' (see Chap. 2). This analyst suggests that greater knowledge of these theories could help to better inform their targeting of network vulnerabilities and assist general decision-making:

> I think I, and probably most analysts in [name of law enforcement agency], could do with more familiarity with the tools and possibly more familiarity with theories. I'm not an avid reader of the most up to date theoretical research on social network analysis but have gone across some of the stuff that suggests where betweenness is more of a factor than say connectedness in determining someone's importance in a network. [...] Simple things like that, I could probably upgrade my understanding of what the network is trying to suggest. (Analyst No. 5)

By having a better understanding of the theories that inform network analysis, this analyst believes that they would be more capable of interpreting the 'outputs' of SNA. This analyst's understanding of network analysis theories is the result of their own initiative to read some of the SNA literature, not from any form of training provided by their organisation (training-related issues are explored further in Chap. 7). This lack of network theory knowledge among analysts is also a reflection of the wider literature. For example, Kennedy and Weimann (2011) suggested that while network theory has been broadly applied to criminal networks by researchers, the relevance of some of the core sociological organisational literature to criminal networks, such as the strength of weak ties theory (see Chap. 2), has failed to be explored in sufficient detail. Similar to the analyst interviewed, Kennedy and Weimann argue that a greater understanding of the underlying network analysis theories will improve the application and interpretation of SNA findings for both researchers and analysts.

Although the use of SNA by analysts is to a large degree a reflection of the literature's focus on disrupting criminal networks, the following section would suggest that this is not necessarily the primary way in which interviewees are using SNA.

Avenues of Enquiry

Despite some analysts using SNA to identify key actors and possible points of vulnerability within criminal networks, SNA is more commonly used to 'suggest avenues of enquiry' (Analyst No. 5). SNA can be used to suggest areas where more information should be collected. As several analysts explained:

> If someone is looking at a small network, say 20 people, and intelligence suggests that there are certain players that hold the key or are central to the network through various other intelligence analytical tools, using SNA could help reveal additional attributes. It may show who is central to the network, which is the degree centrality, and other measures such as closeness centrality and betweenness centrality. Such measures could therefore inform either the investigator or the intelligence analyst to look for other information that they might not have considered before. (Analyst No. 16)

> So, you've maybe got downloads from friends from Facebook or social media or you've got business records and you've got financial records and you've got phone records and you're trying to build up a network [...]. I think it's [SNA] very useful in bringing that together and being able to see some of those connections you might not have seen before or also being able to see across different investigations. [...] It will open up new possibilities for investigative strategies, or I hadn't considered that or I wasn't aware of that sort of thing, and it will do that quickly for us. (Analyst No. 21)

As this last analyst suggests, law enforcement agencies often incorporate phone records or 'call charge records' (CCRs)[3] into their SNA (Berlusconi 2013; Harris-Hogan 2012). SNA based on CCRs may suggest that more information should be obtained on certain actors or previously unknown actors and relationships that may require further attention. As several analysts discuss:

> [SNA]'s just helping you find links that you may not have considered otherwise. (Analyst No. 21)

> Identifying a new person of interest which is a key component of any investigation, who else should we be looking for. More often than not, especially for big complex investigations you're not looking at just one offender, it's usually a collection of people working together and trying to find those people, the new people in that network is probably the single greatest use for [SNA]. It's putting together, going 'I reckon this next person of interest is so and so', and I've been proven right where I've actually done analysis of call data [CCRs] and picked out persons of interest who have subsequently become known offenders. (Analyst No. 2)

This analyst adds that by using SNA to identify further avenues of enquiry it 'can result in better outcomes, quickly resolve a series of offences or better identification of offenders or co-offenders or other persons of interest that would help progress the investigation' (Analyst No. 2).

This is an important finding as it would suggest that despite the extensive academic focus on the ability of SNA to identify structural vulnerabilities in criminal networks (Azad and Gupta 2011; Ball 2016; Bright

---

[3] Call charge records (also called non-content telecommunication) is data that is recorded by telecommunication equipment about communication transactions, such as phone calls, text messages (SMS), and image and video messaging (MMS). These records do not contain the content of the communication but other metadata, such as the date and time of the communication. In Australia, such data can be requested from telecommunication providers with a warrant. According to the Australian Federal Police, such records 'provide important leads for agencies, including evidence of connections and relationships within larger associations over time, evidence of targets' movements and habits, a snapshot of events immediately before and after a crime, evidence to exclude people from suspicion, and evidence needed to obtain warrants for the more intrusive investigative techniques such as interception or access to content. Disclosure of non-content telecommunications data is one of the most efficient and cost effective investigative tools available to law enforcement' (AFP 2012).

et al. 2012, 2015a, b; Cockbain et al. 2011; Duijn and Klerks 2014; Hofmann and Gallupe 2015; Klerks 1999; Koschade 2006; Krebs 2002; Mac Ginty 2010; Malm and Bichler 2011; Morselli 2010; Sparrow 1991), analysts have instead tended to use SNA for the identification of information gaps and persons of interest that detectives were previously unaware of. This does not mean that individuals identified as 'further avenues of enquiry' will not subsequently become targets for disruption, but that based on the interviews conducted, this was not the primary motivation for using SNA. SNA is simply being used to help guide investigative avenues of enquiry and less frequently as a tool in the development of disruption strategies.

Link and Attribute Weights

When it comes to applying SNA, an important decision to make is whether or not to apply some form of strength weighting to either the actors ('attribute weights') and/or to their relationships ('link weights') (Perliger and Pedahzur 2011; Schwartz and Rouselle 2009, p. 192).[4] It remains far more common for link weights not to be used at all and instead to simply record relationships in binary form, whereby a connection exists or not (Bouchard and Konaraski 2014; Bright and Delaney 2013; Morselli 2010; Tsvetovat and Carley 2005). However, if analysts do choose to apply a link weighting there are several ways in which this can be done. Analysts must first identify the different types of relationships that exist, which can include kinship, friendship, religious and economic connections (Bright et al. 2015b; Carley et al. 2003; Cunningham et al. 2013). The link weighting between any two actors

---

[4] The relationships between actors can also be shown as 'directed' and 'undirected' (Ball 2016). Undirected relationships are where they 'logically must always be reciprocated' (Borgatti et al. 2013, p. 12). Directed relationships can either be bi-directional ('operate mutually') or one-directional (as in one actor giving advice to another) (Ball 2016, p. 11; Borgatti and Foster 2003). In a link diagram with directed relationships, the lines connecting the actors will have arrowheads showing the direction of the relationships (or two arrowheads if the relationship is bi-directional). Of the numerous studies that have applied SNA to criminal networks, few have used directed relationships (Bichler et al. 2014; Skillicorn et al. 2014). There was also no mention made by the research participants regarding the use of directed relationships. For these reasons, they will not be examined in this study.

can be measured in several ways, including how recently actors were in contact, the frequency of their contact, the duration of their contact and the 'nature or quality' of their relationship (Coles 2001, p. 590; Granovetter 1973, 1983). For example, if using frequency of contact as the criteria an analyst can apply some form of scaling, such as 1–5, where 1 means very little contact and 5 means very regular contact (see Koschade 2006). These scores can then be entered into an association matrix (see Chap. 2) instead of binary relationships (0 and 1). Several of the research participants incorporate link weightings when applying SNA. The type of weighting predominantly applied by analysts is frequency of contact, which often involves the use of CCRs. As several analysts discussed:

> Okay, a very common area of analysis that we conduct in criminal investigations is to try and measure the relative significance of social relationships in the analysis of call charge records, when they are available. Whether it be a single call charge record for a single individual or we have call charge records, phones used by multiple members of the one group. We frequently make the—or one—of the analyses that are frequently conducted is frequency analysis. How many calls have gone from one handset, from one handset to another? And we presume the most frequently called numbers are the ones, are the ones with the strongest relationships. (Analyst No. 18)

> We often see it if you look at call charge record analysis or analysis of phone calls and things like that. You can often see the hierarchy that a particular network takes on when you look at the frequency of calls between people […]. You will see that there's only contact with a number of people and that sort of contact filters down the line and it sometimes can be quite evident, you can see that [hierarchy] quite clearly. (Analyst No. 20)

As well as CCRs, several analysts found the frequency of financial transactions a useful way of determining the relative importance of a relationship: 'for financial transactions, and any transaction really, it does show you the frequency of [transaction] and they are useful, they help point us in a direction: okay, this is something we might need to look at further' (Analyst No. 21). As well as applying a link weighting based on the frequency of interaction between actors, another analyst described a recent analysis in which they applied a link weighting based on the type of relationship (e.g., family) that existed between actors in the network: 'this one in particular was strength of relationships in terms of positive or negative association. So, stronger weightings for relatives or partners or ethnic links that we know are particularly strong in certain groups, smaller lines for conflict or if the relationship isn't known' (Analyst No. 22). Although link weightings, in particular frequency of connection, do add an extra layer of understanding to an analysis (Koschade 2006), one analyst explained that link weightings do have limitations:

> It [link weighting] has some meaning and it should always be conducted, analysing the cumulative duration of calls to particular numbers […]. [But] if in a given week I've called a particular [phone] number half a dozen times, and another number only twice with the second number I spoke for over an hour on each occasion, that may signal various kinds of relations but it's certainly one that needs further exploration. Is it a girlfriend, spouse, parent? And what's happening in that person's life that leads them to have those lengthy conversations? Is it the significance of that person, is it because they are prevented from being in the same place physically at a particular time? Perhaps because the relationship isn't known to others? So, all those things can be raised in an analysis of duration as well as frequency. (Analyst No. 18)

While this again highlights the dynamic nature of social networks (McIllwain 1999; Medina 2014), the main observation here is that, although a link weighting based on frequency of contact provides further insight, it is insufficient to provide analysts with a full understanding of a network's relationships. A further limitation of link weightings is that a number of the centrality measures commonly applied to criminal networks, including degree centrality, betweenness centrality and closeness centrality, all consider relationships between actors in a network to be of equal value (Bright et al. 2015b; Schwartz and Rouselle 2009). Therefore, regardless of any link weighting that is included, these measures will consider any two actors with the same centrality scores to be of equal importance. There are alternative mathematical computations. For example, *network capital* takes into account the connectedness of a network, the 'potency' of its actors (their ability to access and share resources), and the strength of the relationships in the network (Schwartz and Rouselle 2009, p. 193). However, such computations are more difficult to calculate and are often not available on software that is commonly used by law enforcement agencies, such as Analyst Notebook.[5] Any link weightings applied to a network will often only result in changes to the link diagram. When link weightings are input into analysis software they will visually represent these scores as lines of varying thickness from each individual in the link analysis of that network. The thicker the line the higher that relationship was scored. This relies on a visual interpretation of a link diagram by analysts. As is noted in Chap. 2, however, this can be a flawed process, with analysts easily misinterpreting the findings (McGrath et al. 1997, 2003). Further qualitative data is therefore likely to be needed to develop a greater understanding of the relationship between any two actors. In sum, it was evident from interviewees that link weightings are used occasionally, but as one analyst summarised, in general such 'strength weightings are very rare' (Analyst No. 22).

The second type of weighting, attribute weights, concerns the resources available to an individual, both tangible (such as money, drugs and equipment) and intangible (such as knowledge, skill set and labour) (Bright et al. 2015a). An individual's ability to access such resources is often referred to as their 'network capital' (see Bright et al. 2015a, b; Schwartz and Rouselle 2009; Westlake et al. 2011). Here 'network capital' refers to an individual capacity to access resources. It should not be confused with the mathematical computation *network capital* introduced earlier, which measures the strength of the relationships in a network. Similar to link weightings, some form of scale can be applied to different types of attributes included in the analysis. For example, *labour* might be classified as a 1 and *money* classified as a 5, whereby the latter is considered of greater value to the network. Bright et al. (2015a) argue that it is important to include attribute weightings in a network analysis as it is possible that individuals may not be central to a network (e.g., a low degree centrality

---

[5] Ucinet, for example, is a publicly available network analysis software program that contains many more mathematical computations than Analyst Notebook (Borgatti et al. 2002). Analysts have difficulty accessing such tools for a number of reasons, including monetary constraints and security concerns.

score), but score highly for their ability to access resources, indicating a level of importance to the network. Such individuals are unlikely to be considered important in a network analysis without attribute weightings. The importance of incorporating qualitative data into the analysis of criminal networks was recognised by several of the analysts interviewed. For example, one analyst explained that SNA alone does not provide them with the full picture:

> It [SNA] might be useful, but I would want qualitative data around that, I would want source information to back up certain things […]. It [SNA] can be quite a quantitative thing, you can get quite carried away with going, oh this person is at the core, they're receiving all the phone calls, but it might be that it's not actually connected to the crime that you're investigating. It might be something totally different, it might be a social reason, it might be a different type of crime, like we're investigating a murder but this person contacted you 20 times that night. What did they want? Well they were after drugs and they couldn't get hold of him so that's why they were calling. But it can skew the figures, so you have to go in and look at those exceptions to the rules, you still can't not do analyses on them. It might give you an indicator but you still have to do your job and analyse everything behind it. (Analyst No. 21)

Among those interviewed, however, there was no indication that they were using attribute weightings when applying SNA (see Bright et al. 2015a). This does not mean that analysts were not including qualitative data in their broader analysis of a group, as one analyst explained:

> You use whatever data you have to create a picture. So, if you have enough data to make a chart that suggests a social network, you'll do that as part of your network. But there will also be other data inputs that you may not be able to represent in the chart, health status, things like that may be useful in determining someone's motivation for doing something. So, you'll use all and any information available to you to create an intelligence product. (Analyst No. 5)

However, no mention was made of applying a formalised weighting to such attributes when conducting SNA. This is reflective of the broader literature where it has been noted that researchers and analysts are missing an opportunity to gain further insight into criminal networks by not including attribute weightings (Bright et al. 2015b; Hamill et al. 2008; Hofmann and Gallupe 2015). What the literature has also noted, though, is that there are several reasons why link and attribute weightings are perhaps not applied more regularly (Bright et al. 2015b). First, it can be extremely difficult to obtain accurate relational data that shows who has a relationship with whom, let alone data that contains enough information to apply a link or attribute weighting (data challenges more broadly are explored in Chap. 6) (Berlusconi 2013; Bouchard and Konaraski 2014; Papachristos et al. 2015). For example, law enforcement agencies increasingly see social media as an immensely valuable source of information, including relational data. For example, a study by LexisNexis (2014, p. 2) found that 81 per cent of 'law enforcement professionals' in the US use social media as one source of information during investigations and one quarter use it daily. But as one analyst explained, it is difficult to determine the relative strength of any relationship from social media sources:

> The problem with that is you might call it the Facebook friend, you might be able to see that someone has 200 friends on Facebook [...], but that's a big problem. Trying to identify the strengths of that, it's easy to identify connections through social media but it's difficult to identify the strength of that connection. (Analyst No. 2)

A second reason that link and attribute weightings are used infrequently is that there may be a belief that one type of relationship, such as interpersonal communication, is correlated with other relationships, such as personal friendship. Third, the use of link and attribute weightings will inevitably make the analysis more complicated. These challenges were touched on by several analysts. As one explained: 'you always try and weight them but you're not always able to. You'll start with binary connections' (Analyst No. 5). In addition to the challenges to applying attribute weightings presented by Bright et al. (2015b), one analyst also discussed the manual and time-consuming nature of finding the time to apply such weightings:

When we're talking about a disconnect between the theory and real-world example, that strength of networks is very much covered greatly in theory but trying to get it into our operational side of things is rather difficult […]. To do that you've got to have the tools that make it quick and simple to do and at the moment we don't really have that. We're asking people to sit in there and spend hours going over CCRs and all the rest of it to draw out quantitative links. But then […] the time frames you've got very much limit the amount you can do. You quickly read through calls or you quickly read through what others might have garnered and to try and put that into any reasonable network analysis takes a large amount of time. Then you've got an investigator or at least a sub officer, me, going to my troops, they needed this yesterday, what have we got that we can give them? (Analyst No. 8)

Essentially, the time it takes to apply link or attribute weightings is highly prohibitive and contributes to their infrequent use by analysts. This is a key point of difference between the use of SNA by researchers and the use of SNA in operational environments, where (as this analyst suggests) intelligence reports are time-sensitive, with one impact being that there is often insufficient time to apply link weights.

The use of link and attribute weightings, such as resource attributes, adds a great deal of information to analysis. However, in order to include these aspects of SNA more needs to be done to ensure the availability of necessary data and the tools that allow for the efficient inclusion of such information.

When to Apply Social Network Analysis?

Compounding the lack of understanding about how SNA is being used within ILP, little is known about *when* SNA is being applied. It is not known, for example, whether SNA is most effective when used prior, during or after an investigation. This represents a critical gap in understanding, attributed partly to the fact that the vast majority of the research in this field to date involves retrospective analysis of criminal networks (Everton and Cunningham 2012; Harris-Hogan 2012; Mullins and Dolnik 2010; Natarajan 2006). Among the research participants, there was little consensus as to when SNA should be applied. Based on the discussion earlier in this chapter concerning how SNA is used—specifically its ability to assist with target selection and to identify further avenues of enquiry—it is evident that many of the analysts interviewed look to apply SNA towards the start of an investigation. However, as one analyst explained while discussing an investigation they were involved with, there is a risk that applying SNA towards the start of an investigation will introduce irrelevant data into the analysis and distort the findings:

> If I used it at the beginning of the investigation when I had a lot more phone records involved, and once during the course of the investigation we culled out [phone records], it might have given me a very different picture, but it would have given me the wrong picture if you know what I mean. Because they were also drug dealers and major drug dealers and they spoke to hundreds of people a day. Those specific calls were the calls we were interested in [and] they would have been drowned out by all this other information. (Analyst No. 21)

This 'other information' refers to telephone data connected to actors who are not involved in criminal activities. Analysts and researchers will regularly go through a process of 'cleaning' or 'culling' their data (Carley 2006b, p. 4; Ratcliffe 2002, p. 56). For example, Morselli (2010) went through 270,000 electronic surveillance logs from a police investigation removing irrelevant data, including unanswered calls, busy signals and wrong numbers. According to this analyst, more of this irrelevant data will exist towards the start of an investigation. This would suggest that it is more difficult to establish the boundaries of a network during the early stages of an investigation. However, even if irrelevant information is removed as an investigation progresses, it is unlikely that it will ever be eliminated entirely, meaning irrelevant data is a concern for analysts regardless of when SNA is used.

In contrast, several analysts felt that SNA is better utilised towards the end of an investigation. For example, one analyst explained that when they start to arrest suspects, these individuals will sometimes reveal information about relationships and actors involved in the targeted network that were previously unknown to them and to investigators:

In many types of investigations, the target of our investigation is totally unaware, or ideally, is totally unaware of our interest in them. But at a certain point when they are arrested they will be offered the opportunity being interviewed about the crime that they have been involved in. And they may talk about relationships or interactions with other people who we previously weren't aware of or they may offer up valid information about the relative significance of those people. Which is worthwhile information but was not available during the targeting phase of the investigation. (Analyst No. 18)

This would suggest that in instances where arrested suspects provide new information about the targeted network, analysts should apply or re-apply SNA to determine if the investigation should focus on any other actors. Directly related to this, several analysts felt SNA should be used once an investigation is over as they are likely to have more of the data they actually want: '[SNA]'s best done after an investigation is complete. [...] By definition you will have more data' (Analyst No. 18).[6] SNA can be used as a way of evaluating the investigation as a whole, with a particular focus on those who were targeted. Furthermore, law enforcement agencies can set up future investigations by identifying new targets or further avenues of enquiry. Using SNA to help guide future investigations also logically follows, given that investigations are rarely mutually exclusive. As one analyst explained:

One investigation is not entirely isolated from others. There will have been other investigations that have occurred or might still be running that involves some of those participants. So, the analysis that is possible, that can be done in the nature of social network analysis, takes into account those prior investigations and those criminal networks who we know [...] are likely to be those where some of the participants had been involved in recent prior investigations. (Analyst No. 18)

---

[6] For the purposes of this study an investigation is regarded as over when a brief of evidence is handed to public prosecutors. A brief of evidence is a collection of documents, including statements (from the police, victims and any witnesses), copies of any exhibits (such photos) and a transcript of an interview between the suspect and police that is handed over by the latter to prosecutors to use as potential evidence should they proceed to trial (NSW Government 2017).

However, using SNA to help evaluate the decisions made in an investigation (as well as setting up future ones) is not how interviewees are currently using SNA. It is one analyst's belief that the opportunity to use SNA in this way is currently being missed:

> I think we could do so much more with it [SNA] and probably get some really good conclusions out of it and set us up for future investigations a lot more. But we tend to be very traditional in the way that we look at the outcomes. [...] When we finish an investigation we just go, yep, box it up, put that over there, let's just forget about it and never go back to it again. When really that's the time when we should be going back and be doing those little extra bits of network analysis that either prove the way that we were looking at it was right or show us where we were going wrong, learn those lessons and be able to use those in the next one [investigation]. (Analyst No. 8)

By applying SNA at the end of an investigation to evaluate prior decision-making, with a particular focus on the development of future investigations, analysts would be using SNA to guide strategic decision-making within their organisations, rather than limiting its use to tactical intelligence. Several analysts felt that SNA should be used 'constantly' throughout an investigation. Interviewees gave no approximation as to the frequency with which they apply SNA throughout the course of investigations. However, one analyst explained that SNA should be re-applied each time new relational data comes in, and that in doing so they can determine the value of that new information:

> Well, you can update as an investigation progresses, so that's bringing in new information [...]. Often what I will do is I will have my big ongoing chart and then it might be all one colour, blue, and then what I will do is have a new bit of information come in and I'll plot on a new worksheet and change all the links to red. I'll then cut and paste those two things together and then all you need to do is look for where blue meets red, if there is no connection then it will just be a blue blob and a red blob. But if there is, then what happens with Analyst Notebook it will join the links over and then you hit the rearrange chart icon and it will rearrange its format and then you will be able see how the blue links join to the red links. It helps you to visually understand things like that. (Analyst No. 2)

Using SNA throughout an investigation would be a step towards overcoming the dynamic nature of social networks and one of the major limitations of SNA. However, actually applying SNA in this way is extremely difficult (Chap. 4 discusses this issue in greater detail, while Chap. 6 examines the varied nature of investigations, such as their size and length). A final point in the criminal justice system where SNA is sometimes used is in court. It has been noted that law enforcement within the UK (Cockbain et al. 2011) and US (Carter 2009) regularly present link diagrams of criminal networks in court rooms. Cockbain et al. (2011) suggest that SNA is an effective way of demonstrating criminal network structures to a court. According to one analyst, they will often apply SNA towards the end of an investigation so it can be presented in court: 'generally we do our AN [Analyst Notebook] charts when it comes to court, it's at the tail end [of an investigation]' (Analyst No. 14). However, several analysts highlighted that trying to present the findings of SNA in a courtroom can be highly problematic. Creating a link diagram to guide an investigation versus one that is admissible in court are two very different tasks. As several analysts explained:

> The limitations are that we can only use it for intel gathering purposes. At this stage, it really can't be used as evidence, its more for information gathering. (Analyst No. 26)

> There's obviously a big difference between evidence and intelligence. What I'm saying is if it's something that's black and white and can be proven, it can be evidentiary based. Most of what we do is based on probability and likelihood, so it can always be questioned, but it could be the best guess or it could be 90% probability etc. […] Quite often for intelligence what we do, it doesn't end up being used in court, very little. Network analysis, if someone was to prepare something to be used for court, it could be, but it would have to be quite precise. (Analyst No. 3)

As these analysts suggest, the outputs of SNA are often helpful in guiding both theirs and the detectives' enquiries, but would rarely meet the standards of admissible evidence for a trial. According to one analyst, another issue with presenting the results of SNA in court is that they may not be understood by all involved, particularly some of the more technical aspects such as the mathematical computations:

We [analysts] are analytically trained. Investigators are trained differently, bosses are trained, management is trained differently and again as I say lawyers might think they understand it [but] I'm not sure that they all do. I'm sure some do, but conveying it to the ultimate decision-makers, [that] being the jury, it might look flashy, […] but if it's not understood, being flash and meaning only something to one small [group of] analytical people doesn't get [you] what you're trying to get. (Analyst No. 13)

This would suggest that even if the standards of admissibility are met, analysts are reluctant to present an SNA of a criminal group in court fearing that it may not be understood by the lawyers, and critically, by the jury. It is evident there are both strengths and limitations with using SNA before, during and after an investigation, as well as in the broader criminal justice system, and it is critical that analysts are aware of these and how they will impact on their use of SNA. Overall, a general view of SNA among interviewees is perhaps summarised best by one analyst: 'At this point in time I […] see it [SNA] as a valuable tool which has largely been underutilised' (Analyst No. 16).

Conclusion

This chapter has examined how SNA is being used within crime intelligence. It was found that while some analysts still used first- and second-generation network analysis tools, most had at least tried using SNA, with many claiming to use it regularly. The chapter also found that similarly to the broader literature, some analysts were using SNA to try and identify structural vulnerabilities within criminal networks. However, an important discovery was that SNA was being used by research participants predominantly as a tool for identifying information gaps and persons of interest that were previously unknown to detectives. It was clear that while interviewees recognised the importance of qualitative data, they found it difficult to incorporate this information into an analysis by way of using link and attribute weightings. Finally, it was found that there was no consensus among research participants about when it is most appropriate to use SNA—whether prior, during or after an investigation. The following chapter examines the more commonly discussed challenges of applying SNA, the 'characteristics of criminal networks'.

References

AFP, *Telecommunications data retention – an overview* (Parliament of Australia, 2012). http://www.aph.gov.au/About_Parliament/Parliamentary_Departments/Parliamentary_Library/pubs/BN/2012-2013/DataRetention#_Toc338835111. Accessed 6 July 2017

S. Azad, A. Gupta, A quantitative assessment on 26/11 Mumbai attack using social network analysis. J. Terrorism Res. **2**(2), 4–14 (2011)

L. Ball, Automating social network analysis: a power tool for counter-terrorism. Secur. J. **29**(2), 147–168 (2016)

G. Berlusconi, Do all the pieces matter? Assessing the reliability of law enforcement data sources for the network analysis of wire taps. Global Crime **14**(1), 61–81 (2013)

G. Bichler, S. Lim, E. Larin, Tactical social network analysis: using affiliation networks to aid serial homicide investigation. Homicide Stud. **21**(2), 133–158 (2016)

G. Bichler, A. Malm, J. Enriquez, Magnetic facilities: identifying key juvenile convergence places with social network analysis. Crime Delinq. **60**(7), 971–998 (2014)

S. Borgatti, M. Everett, J.C. Johnson, *Analyzing social networks* (SAGE Publications, London, 2013)

S.P. Borgatti, M.G. Everett, L.C. Freeman, *Ucinet for Windows: software for social network analysis* (2002). https://sites.google.com/site/ucinetsoftware/home. Accessed 26 September 2012

S.P. Borgatti, P.P. Foster, The network paradigm in organizational research: a review and typology. J. Manage. **29**(6), 991–1013 (2003)

M. Bouchard, J. Amirault, Advances in research on illicit networks. Global Crime **14**(2–3), 119–122 (2013)

M. Bouchard, R. Konaraski, Assessing the core membership of a youth gang from its co-offending network, in *Crime and networks*, ed. by C. Morselli, (Routledge, New York, 2014), pp. 81–93

D.A. Bright, J.J. Delaney, Evolution of a drug trafficking network: mapping changes in network structure and function across time. Global Crime **14**(2–3), 238–260 (2013)

D.A. Bright, C. Greenhill, M. Reynolds, A. Ritter, C. Morselli, The use of actor-level attributes and centrality measures to identify key actors: a case study of an Australian drug trafficking network. J. Contemp. Crim. Justice **31**(3), 262–278 (2015a)

D.A. Bright, C. Greenhill, A. Ritter, C. Morselli, Networks within networks: using multiple link types to examine network structure and identify key actors in a drug trafficking operation. Global Crime **16**(3), 1–19 (2015b)

D.A. Bright, C.E. Hughes, J. Chalmers, Illuminating dark networks: a social network analysis of an Australian drug trafficking syndicate. Crime Law Soc. Chang. **57**(2), 151–176 (2012)

R. Burt, *Structural holes: the social structure of competition* (Harvard University Press, Cambridge, 1992)

K.M. Carley, Destabilization of covert networks. Comput. Math. Org. Theor. **12**(1), 51–66 (2006a)

K.M. Carley, *A dynamic network approach to the assessment of terrorist groups and the impact of alternative courses of action*, Paper presented to Visualising Network Information, Neuilly-sur-Seine, France, 2006b

K.M. Carley, M. Dombroski, M. Tsvetovat, J. Reminga, N. Kamneva, *Destabilizing dynamic covert networks*, Paper presented to Proceedings of the 8th International Command and Control Research and Technology Symposium, National Defense War College, Washington, DC, 2003

D.L. Carter, *Law enforcement intelligence: a guide for state, local, and tribal law enforcement agencies* (2009), No. 24 July 2012. https://it.ojp.gov/documents/d/e050919201-IntelGuide_web.pdf. Accessed 21 August 2018

E. Cockbain, H. Brayley, G. Laycock, Exploring internal child sex trafficking networks using social network analysis. Policing **5**(2), 144–157 (2011)

N. Coles, It's not what you know it's who you know: analysing serious crime groups as social networks. Br. J. Criminol. **41**(4), 580–594 (2001)

D. Cunningham, S. Everton, G. Wilson, C. Padilla, D. Zimmerman, Brokers and key players in the internationalization of the FARC. Stud. Conflict Terrorism **36**(6), 477–502 (2013)

D. Décary-Hétu, B. Dupont, The social network of hackers. Global Crime **13**(3), 160–175 (2012)

P.A.C. Duijn, V. Kashirin, P.M.A. Sloot, The relative ineffectiveness of criminal network disruption. Sci. Rep. **4**(4238), 1–15 (2014)

P.A.C. Duijn, P.P.H.M. Klerks, Social network analysis applied to criminal networks: recent developments in Dutch law enforcement, in *Networks and network analysis for defence and security*, ed. by A. J. Masys, (Springer, Heidelberg, 2014), pp. 121–159

B. Dupont, Security networks and counter-terrorism: a reflection on the limits of adversarial isomorphism, in *Social networks, terrorism and counter-terrorism: radical and connected*, ed. by M. Bouchard, (Routledge, London, 2015), pp. 155–174

S.F. Everton, D. Cunningham, Detecting significant changes in dark networks. Behav. Sci. Terrorism Polit. Aggression **5**(2), 1–21 (2012)

M. Granovetter, The strength of weak ties. Am. J. Sociol. **78**(6), 1360–1380 (1973)

M. Granovetter, The strength of weak ties: a network theory revisited. Sociol. Theor. **1**, 201–233 (1983)

J.T. Hamill, R.F. Deckro, J.W. Chrissis, R.F. Mills, Analysis of layered social networks. Isophere **Winter**, 27–33 (2008)

W.R. Harper, D.H. Harris, The application of link analysis to police intelligence. Hum. Factors **17**(2), 157–164 (1975)

S. Harris-Hogan, Anatomy of a terrorist cell: a study of the network uncovered in Sydney in 2005. Behav. Sci. Terrorism Polit. Aggression **5**(2), 1–18 (2012)

D.C. Hofmann, O. Gallupe, Leadership protection in drug-trafficking networks. Global Crime **16**(2), 123–138 (2015)

J.A. Johnson, J.D. Reitzal, *Social network analysis in an operational environment: defining the utility of a network approach for crime analysis using the Richmond City Police Department as a case study* (2011). http://www.coginta.org/en/document/policy_working_paper_series?page=3. Accessed 8 August 2012

M.R. Kebbell, D.A. Muller, K. Martin, Understanding and managing bias, in *Dealing with uncertainties in policing serious crime*, ed. by G. Bammer, (Australian National University E Press, Canberra, 2010)

J. Kennedy, G. Weimann, The strength of weak terrorist ties. Terrorism Polit. Violence **23**(2), 201–212 (2011)

M. Kenney, The architecture of drug trafficking: network forms of organisation in the Colombian cocaine trade. Global Crime **8**(3), 233–259 (2007)

P. Klerks, The network paradigm applied to criminal organisations: theoretical nitpicking or relevant doctrine for investigators? Recent developments in the Netherlands. Connections **24**(3), 53–65 (1999)

S. Koschade, A social network analysis of Jemaah Islamiyah: the applications to counterterrorism and intelligence. Stud. Conflict Terrorism **29**(6), 559–575 (2006)

V. Krebs, Mapping networks of terrorist cells. Connections **24**(3), 43–52 (2002)

C. Leuprecht, A. Aulthouse, O. Walther, The puzzling resilience of transnational organized criminal networks. Police Pract. Res. **17**(4), 376–387 (2016)

LexisNexis, Social media use in law enforcement: crime prevention and investigative activities continue to drive usage. *LexisNexis* (2014). http://www.lexisnexis.com/risk/downloads/whitepaper/2014-social-media-use-in-law-enforcement.pdf. Accessed 9 January 2017

R. Mac Ginty, Social network analysis and counterinsurgency: a counterproductive strategy? Crit. Stud. Terrorism **3**(2), 209–226 (2010)

E.D. Mainas, The analysis of criminal and terrorist organisations as social network structures: a quasi-experimental study. Int. J. Police Sci. Manage. **14**(3), 264–283 (2012)

A. Malm, G. Bichler, Networks of collaborating criminals: assessing the structural vulnerability of drug markets. J. Res. Crime Delinq. **48**(2), 271–297 (2011)

C. McGrath, J. Blythe, D. Krackhardt, The effect of spatial arrangement on judgments and errors in interpreting graphs. Soc. Networks **19**(3), 223–242 (1997)

C. McGrath, D. Krackhardt, J. Blythe, Visualizing complexity in networks: seeing both the forest and the trees. Connections **25**(1), 37–47 (2003)

J.S. McIllwain, Organized crime: a social network approach. Crime Law Soc. Chang. **32**(4), 301–323 (1999)

R.M. Medina, Social network analysis: a case study of the Islamist terrorist network. Secur. J. **27**(1), 97–121 (2014)

C. Morselli, Assessing vulnerable and strategic positions in a criminal network. J. Contemp. Crim. Justice **26**(4), 382–392 (2010)

C. Morselli (ed.), *Crime and networks* (Routledge, New York, 2014)

S. Mullins, A. Dolnik, An exploratory, dynamic application of social network analysis for modelling the development of Islamist terror cells in the West. Behav. Sci. Terrorism Polit. Aggression **2**(1), 3–29 (2010)

M. Natarajan, Understanding the structure of a large heroin distribution network: a quantitative analysis of qualitative data. J. Quant. Criminol. **22**(2), 171–192 (2006)

NSW Government, *Reading a brief of evidence* (NSW Government, 2017). http://www.lawaccess.nsw.gov.au/Pages/representing/driving_offences_and_crime/pleading_not_guilty/preparing_for_the_hearing/reading_a_brief_of_evidence.aspx. Accessed 31 July 2017

A.V. Papachristos, C. Wildeman, E. Roberto, Tragic, but not random: the social contagion of nonfatal gunshot injuries. Soc. Sci. Med. **125**, 139–150 (2015)

A. Perliger, A. Pedahzur, Social network analysis in the study of terrorism and political violence. Polit. Sci. Polit. **44**(2), 45–50 (2011)

J. Ratcliffe, Intelligence-led policing and the problems of turning rhetoric into practice. Polic. Soc. **12**(1), 53–66 (2002)

J. Ratcliffe, *Intelligence-led policing* (Routledge, New York, 2016)

N. Roberts, S.F. Everton, Strategies for combating dark networks. J. Soc. Struct. **12**(2), 1–32 (2011)

D.K. Rossmo, *Criminal investigative failures* (CRC Press, New York, 2009)

D.M. Schwartz, T. Rouselle, Using social network analysis to target criminal networks. Trends Org. Crime **12**(2), 188–207 (2009)

D.B. Skillicorn, Q. Zheng, C. Morselli, Modeling dynamic social networks using spectral embedding. Soc. Network Anal. Min. **4**(1), 182 (2014)

M.K. Sparrow, The application of network analysis to criminal intelligence: an assessment of the prospects. Soc. Networks **13**(3), 251–274 (1991)

M. Tsvetovat, K.M. Carley, *Structural knowledge and success of anti-terrorist activity: the downside of structural equivalence* (Carnegie Mellon University, 2005). http://repository.cmu.edu/isr/43. Accessed 21 May 2012

R. van der Hulst, Introduction to social network analysis (SNA) as an investigative tool. Trends Org. Crime **12**(2), 101–121 (2009)

B.G. Westlake, M. Bouchard, R. Frank, Finding the key players in online child exploitation networks. Policy Internet **3**(2), 1–32 (2011)

4

Social Network Analysis and the Characteristics of Criminal Networks

Introduction

The focus for this chapter is on what Sparrow (1991) describes as the 'characteristics of criminal networks'. Sparrow (1991, p. 261) recognised that 'most network analysis tools have been developed within the context of retrospective social science investigations, and they are therefore designed for use on networks which are small, static, and with very few distinct types of linkages (generally only one)'. As shown in Chap. 2, however, criminal networks vary in size, are far from static and have relationships of varying types (Bakker et al. 2012; Burcher and Whelan 2015; Charette and Papachristos 2017). Because of this, Sparrow (1991) identified several unique challenges that complicate the application of existing network analysis approaches to criminal databases.

Sparrow identified four 'characteristics of criminal networks' that would make applying social network analysis (SNA) to criminal groups challenging: the *size* of criminal databases, the *incompleteness* of data, the *fuzzy boundaries* of a network and the *dynamic* nature of social networks. Since Sparrow's (1991) seminal paper, several other 'data challenges' have been recognised alongside incompleteness of criminal network data,

© The Author(s) 2020
M. Burcher, *Social Network Analysis and Law Enforcement*, Crime Prevention and Security Management, https://doi.org/10.1007/978-3-030-47771-4_4

including *incorrectness, inconsistences* and *data transformation*. These four characteristics, including the broader category of data challenges, have been regarded by researchers as the primary challenges of applying SNA to criminal networks (Duijn and Klerks 2014; Malm et al. 2008; Yuan et al. 2013). This chapter examines these and other challenges by drawing on the experiences of crime intelligence analysts in their attempts to apply SNA to criminal networks.

Size

Size refers to how large criminal intelligence databases can be and the fact that it may be difficult to process such datasets. Perspective on the size of the increase in global data production is evident in IBM's estimation, in 2011, that 90 per cent of the world's data had been produced in the preceding two years alone (IBM 2011). In the context of global increases in data production, it is understandable that the size of criminal intelligence databases has increased substantially (Ratcliffe 2002; Sheptycki 2017). Law enforcement agencies now collect data from 'traditional' sources, such as physical surveillance, paper trails (e.g. financial records) and telephone intercepts, as well as newer sources, including emails, text messages, computer hard drives and instant messaging (or IM)[1] (Décary-Hétu and Dupont 2012, p. 162). Interviewees highlighted this change, with one senior analyst suggesting that at an organisational level there is a strong push for analysts to obtain information from as many sources as possible:

> We teach through our program a lot in relation to collection and collation, so in that collection/collation process there are a lot of data sources that need to be considered. So, into that social networking we would be expecting them [analysts] to look at the avenues of enquiry that identify perhaps those types of social footprints online, whether it be online, through social media, whether it be through normal telecommunication type platforms.

---

[1] IM is a form of online chat that uses the internet for real-time text communication. IM apps, which can be used on cell phones or computers, are the end-user applications that facilitate this communication.

So, within that space or sphere of analysing data or information, whether it be looking at crime data, whether it be looking at data in relation to persons of interest, we would be expecting them to draw out those types of information that would potentially activate other avenues of enquiry to find that type of information that we could draw into that social network analysis. (Analyst No. 17)

By collecting information from so many sources 'the age of "big data" has come to policing' (Joh 2014, p. 35). While there is no universally agreed-upon definition of big data, generally speaking it refers to 'the emergence of new datasets with massive volume that change at a rapid pace, are very complex, and exceed the reach of the analytical capabilities of commonly used hardware environments and software tools for data management' (Akhgar et al. 2015, p. 3). At present, this includes databases that contain terabytes (1000 gigabytes), petabytes (1000 terabytes) and even zettabytes (1,000,000 petabytes) of data.

Almost all of those interviewed expressed a general concern about the information technology (IT) systems available to them (explored further in Chap. 7) and several had specific concerns about the capacity of their software packages to process large quantites of data when conducting SNA. As several analysts explained:

From an operational point of view, probably still the biggest thing to us is that we've probably got access to a major amount of information that we're not able to fully assess properly and that's more down to the tools that we've got to assess it with. (Analyst No. 8)

You are constrained by the power of the software. I've nearly broken Analyst Notebook. I did ring them [software developers] up and ask, how much [data] can I actually put in? (Analyst No. 2)

According to Akhgar et al. (2015, p. 102), Analyst Notebook and other analytical programs popular with law enforcement, including Palantir and SPSS, are incapable of handling even 'one-thousandth' of the information that would be considered 'big data'. Not all criminal databases would meet the definition of 'big data', but it is evident that when conducting SNA, there are restrictions on the quantity of data analysts can include due to the processing limitations of the software available to them. This would suggest there are limits on the 'size' of the criminal networks that analysts can examine (research participants were comfortable with broadly discussing the processing limitations of their software but were unwilling to state specifically what these limits are, citing security concerns). In this instance, size refers to both the number of actors/relationships included in the analysis and the volume of data about the network, including actor characteristics and relationship types.

Research participants also expressed several other concerns with the size of their criminal databases and how size can impact on their ability to use SNA. For example, one analyst suggested that it can be difficult to visually display large networks: 'when you have a huge amount of data it can look like a ball of string, so at the end of the day it's not really useful to present as a picture, you have to analyse it; when you have a lot of data it just can't be presented in its entirety' (Analyst No. 3). This does not mean that the link diagram component of SNA should be dismissed entirely. It is still regarded as a very useful way of presenting the results of an analysis (Strang 2014; Tayebi and Glasser 2016), for example in instances such as an analyst presenting their findings to a detective (discussed further in Chap. 6). There are also some instances where a visual inspection of a link diagram is the preferred method of analysis over mathematical computations. An example of this would be applying SNA to a small network on multiple occasions, where any changes in the network's structure would easily be seen from a visual inspection of the link diagram (see Mullins and Dolnik 2010). Overall though, this analyst's view of SNA would support the notion that once a network reaches a certain size the link diagram component becomes rather meaningless, in which case it becomes necessary to apply suitable mathematical computations (Bichler et al. 2016; Colladon and Remondi 2017; Johnson and Reitzal 2011; Roberts and Everton 2011).

Another concern with large criminal databases, as one analyst discussed, is that there is ultimately a trade-off because although 'intelligence analysts will want more information, [...] that can also create a great deal of distraction' (Analyst No. 5). SNA is already regarded as a time-consuming process (Bright et al. 2015b; Kriegler 2014; Xu and

Chen 2005); as the quantity of information increases, the time it will take analysts to 'clean' the data also increases (see data transformation below). Software packages have developed considerably over the past two and a half decades, making data processing far more 'user-friendly' (Duijn and Klerks 2014, p. 150). However, in this time the rate of data collection and retention by law enforcement agencies has also rapidly increased (Brodeur and Dupont 2006; Décary-Hétu and Dupont 2012; Hutchins and Benham-Hutchins 2010; Sheptycki 2000). The impact of this massive push within law enforcement agencies to continually collect more data means that they have exceeded their ability to fully analyse this information. Analysts are unable to analyse networks that are above a certain size and thus cannot use SNA to its full potential.

Data Challenges

The second characteristic of criminal networks identified by Sparrow (1991) is the *incompleteness* of criminal databases. Since then several other issues that can be placed under the umbrella term 'data challenges' have been identified as impediments to the accuracy and efficiency of SNA. They are *incorrectness*, *inconsistency* and *data transformation* (Morris and Deckro 2013; Xu and Chen 2005).

Incompleteness

Criminal network data will inevitably be incomplete due to some actors, their relationships and the characteristics of those connections going unobserved or unrecorded by law enforcement (Malm and Bichler 2011; Medina 2014; Saidi et al. 2017). Incomplete data can distort the outputs of SNA (Décary-Hétu and Dupont 2012; Hofmann and Gallupe 2015). For example, it may be that an individual that has a low-centrality score (indicating they have few relationships with other actors) is in fact well connected to the rest of the network, but that these relationships have simply gone unobserved. Most interviewees identified incomplete data as a core challenge of applying SNA to criminal networks. As several analysts discuss:

> Social networks or the absence of social networks doesn't say that there is no connection there, it just says that we can't see a connection there. So, there's some blind spots. (Analyst No. 19)

> I think it's [limitations of SNA] the initial data inputs. The tools are great, the theories are great, but you don't always have access to the amount of information on a given individual or given group that would make those tools and theories effective. (Analyst No. 5)

> We really don't have too much to base those [SNA] assessments on. Using just the [name of this organisations primary criminal database] system which is only going to show people seen together at the same time, spoken to at the same time, somebody, some cop somewhere happened to think they were connected in some way. Sometimes the information that we have got to assess is not great. (Analyst No. 25)

Although it was noted in Chap. 2 that the mathematical computations used in SNA are relatively robust to missing data (up to 10 per cent missing), these analysts suggest that their criminal databases are often too incomplete to conduct SNA. While there are numerous factors that contribute to the incompleteness of criminal network data, one is the biases that exist within the investigative methodologies used by law enforcement (Bright et al. 2012; Burcher and Whelan 2017; Duijn and Sloot 2015; Frank 1978; Ratcliffe and Sheptycki 2004).[2] For example, mathematical computations can be distorted by the amount of data collected on particular individuals. This can occur when police collect large amounts of data about certain actors, not because they are necessarily central to the targeted network, but as a result of focusing their attention

---

[2] Sometimes called organisational or institutional bias (Gunnell et al. 2016; Ratcliffe and Sheptycki 2004), investigative bias should not be confused with the issue of 'cognitive bias' discussed in Chap. 3. Investigative bias is also separate from 'bias crimes' which can be defined as 'a criminal offence committed against persons, associates of persons, property or society that is motivated, in whole or in part, by an offender's bias against an individual's or group's actual or perceived; race, religion, ethnic/national origin, sex/gender, gender identity, age, disability status, sexual orientation and homeless status' (Mullane 2015, p. 5).

on these individuals more than the rest of the network (Bright et al. 2012). A further example of investigative bias, as one analyst explained, occurs when police are conducting surveillance operations and those being targeted may only be under surveillance at certain times of the day due to resource constraints and because of the inability of law enforcement to access certain locations:

> Sometimes we learn about relationships we were previously unaware of through the physical surveillance of criminal targets. That surveillance may also be not uniform [complete surveillance coverage] in that it happens at certain times of the day, more likely than others. It might be that those relationships involving people who have met in certain circumstances in public spaces versus buildings we don't have access to, might also colour that picture that's developed of the social relationships. [...] But whether they form a representative picture of the most significant relationships that person has, or a complete picture. It's possible in some families that are constantly interacting with the police that we have that picture. But it's likely in many others that we have nothing like the full picture and we may not have the most significant relationships recorded at all. (Analyst No. 18)

According to this analyst, when surveillance is not 'uniform' it is likely that they are not capturing a 'complete picture' of the targeted network. This task is even more challenging when criminal groups employ counter-surveillance measures, such as having local residents or family alert the group of 'unusual police activity in the neighbourhood' (Spapens 2011, p. 30). While it is unlikely that police will ever have complete surveillance or a complete picture of the networks they are investigating, this highlights how the choices they make around who they focus their attention on will introduce a degree of bias into the information they collect. The same analyst also suggested that incomplete or 'unrepresentative data' can be the result of using information from previous investigations that was not collected with the objective of conducting SNA:

> When we are talking about unrepresentative data samples as well, we need to be aware when we are collecting data for a purpose directly related to building a picture of the social network of the target, versus data that was collected with some other objective in mind, that data collected more gen-

erally will have an application in social network analysis but the amount of bias in it or the completeness of it will differ. Sometimes we are collecting data in one mode at one stage of an investigation and then move to another mode, but we treat the entire data pool as being accessible, as it should be, for social network analysis without taking into account that there was a bias in the collection at one phase. (Analyst No. 18)

The point here is that many of the data sources used by law enforcement agencies, including surveillance and previous investigations, are likely to be incomplete due to varying degrees of investigative bias. This reinforces a common finding of this study that decision-making, particularly with regard to target selection, should not be based solely on the findings of SNA, and instead should be used alongside other forms of intelligence analysis to influence this process. Other forms of analysis that are likely to pair well with SNA include crime script analysis (Bright 2017; Duijn and Klerks 2014; Morselli and Roy 2008), geographical information systems (or GIS) (Ratcliffe 2004) and criminal business profiles (NCIS 2000).

Despite investigative bias being a key concern for the research participants, the investigative methods employed by law enforcement agencies may not have much of an impact on SNA (Berlusconi 2013; Bright 2015; Bright et al. 2015a). For example, a study by Bright et al. (2015a), which applied SNA to an Australian drug-trafficking network, found that despite the fact that the data they had used was from the police files of only two individuals in the network, they were not always the actors that had the highest centrality scores, as might have been expected. So although the police primarily focused their attention on these two actors, the data they collected did not appear to distort the centrality measures applied. Bright et al. (2015a) concluded that this inherent bias in the data used could not account for all results. Therefore, police files focused on particular individuals may contain sufficient information about co-offenders so as not to skew findings to the point where they are unusable. While this gives a degree of confidence to analysts that the biases that exist within their investigations may not impact on the findings of SNA, further research is required to fully understand this issue.

Interviewees also noted that criminal databases are often incomplete due to poor data entry standards. For example, one analyst explained that they are often left with incomplete data internally because officers do not always fill out reports completely: 'sometimes you can get incomplete parts of the puzzle and information reports that aren't filled out completely, so you're missing bits and pieces' (Analyst No. 21). Poor data entry standards are explained, in part, by the increased collection of data discussed earlier in the chapter. For example, according to Victoria Police, 50 per cent of an officer's time during each shift is actually spent on various tasks associated with information capture and reporting (Victoria Police 2014). It is not clear, however, to what extent officers fail to fill out forms completely. Again, this is an area that requires greater examination as the extent of the problem may vary in different areas within law enforcement agencies and each jurisdiction.

Incorrectness

A further data challenge is that collected relational data can be incorrect, a factor which can, in turn, affect the outputs of SNA (Morris and Deckro 2013). Xu and Chen (2005) suggested that incorrect data, such as information about an offender's identity, physical characteristics or address, is often the result of either data entry errors by law enforcement officers or intentional deception from offenders. The deliberate supply of misinformation is arguably the most challenging source of incorrect data and the greatest difference between 'bright' and 'dark' networks. Dark networks refer to groups that 'operate covertly and illegally' (Bakker et al. 2012, p. 4). Bright or 'light' networks are those not engaged in criminal activities (Everton and Cunningham 2015; Morris and Deckro 2013), such as sports or social clubs. A common form of misinformation involves offenders using multiple aliases or nicknames to mask their identity. This issue is explained by several analysts:

> The other limitations are obviously privacy and naming conventions. For the majority of social media sites that I've seen, there doesn't appear to be any rock-solid verification procedure. I could establish a social media pro-

file under the name of Bill Blogs and I've got a phone that I bought from Safeway [a supermarket] for $50 and used the name Bill Blogs to activate the phone and there's my whole verification procedure. There's nothing that actually verifies who someone actually is. (Analyst No. 1)

Nine out of 10 guys will not use their correct name, they would be an idiot if they did. So, you're getting things like nicknames. (Analyst No. 10)

This will of course depend on the data source being used. As these analysts suggest, many social media sites do not have an identity verification process. However, other sources commonly used by law enforcement, such as financial records obtained from a bank, will generally have stricter verification processes. The main point here is that a problem arises for law enforcement agencies when they incorrectly record each aliases/nickname as separate actors and not as the same person. Therefore, when an analyst applies SNA, the network will appear larger than it actually is due to the counting of an actor multiple times. It will also reduce the importance or centrality of an actor due to their relationships being split across multiple identities (Malm et al. 2010).

One analyst noted that it is common practice within law enforcement agencies to apply a reliability and validity weighting in an effort to reduce the chances of incorrect data entering an analysis:

That's where you use a weighting to describe the reliability of a piece of information. So, you'll give it an assignment of a number and a letter, A1 being the most reliable, F6 being the least reliable. That's a formal way and commonly used in intelligence analysis practice to describe the reliability of information by which you're determining a connection. Sometimes that's not available, so you would make an informal call on the weighting, if it's single source, so you've only got the connection from one particular intelligence input. It's less reliable than if you have multiple sources, preferably three sources says a connection is good and more than that the better. (Analyst No. 5)

As this analyst explained, a reliability and validity weighting is a determination on the trustworthiness and accuracy of certain information. While there are a variety of reliability and validity weightings used within the intelligence field, in this instance the letter designates the reliability of the source ('A' being most reliable and 'F' being an untested source) and the number represents a determination on the validity of the information ('1' means that the information is known to be true and '6' that the information is likely to be false). According to Carter (2009), reliability and validity weightings also play an important role in resource allocation. Using a simplified example, Carter (2009) explained that if a law enforcement agency receives information about a possible terrorist attack, but that information has a very low reliability and validity weighting, little credibility will be placed on the threat. Alternatively, as 'validity and reliability increase, the greater credibility will result in devoting more resources to corroboration and a response' (Carter 2009, p. 163). However, there currently is no convenient way to incorporate reliability and validity weightings into SNA (van der Hulst 2009). For intelligence analysts with access to Analyst Notebook it is possible to classify the relationships in a network as 'confirmed', 'unconfirmed' and 'tentative'. One analyst discussed their use of this function:

> [I] have used whether it's a confirmed or unconfirmed connection. So just because people are seen in a building doesn't necessarily mean they're there together. So, that's helped in the past and that comes into when you're doing your analysis to take into account that sort of thing. That's what the program will give you but you have to analyse it yourself. (Analyst No. 23)

This approach, however, still fails to take into account the complexity of the reliability and validity weightings commonly used by law enforcement agencies. Exploring how such weightings can be better included in SNA should be the focus of future research. Nevertheless, such weightings as they currently stand are an effective way of outlining the reliability and validity of the data used. It is for this reason that researchers may benefit from incorporating a reliability and validity weighting into their applications of SNA to criminal networks.

Researchers broadly discuss the reliability and validity of the data they use and highlight any limitations (Berlusconi 2013; Duijn and Klerks 2014; Malm et al. 2008; Varese 2013), but they mostly do not apply a formal weighting similar to those used by law enforcement agencies. For example, Duijn et al. (2014) split their data into two groups, 'dataset hard' and 'dataset soft', to indicate the relative reliability and validity of their data. However, this is still simplistic compared with the system discussed by Analyst No. 5 above (A1-F6), which involves a total of 36 possible categories regarding the reliability and validity of a piece of information. Researchers make an assumption that data that has already passed through the hands of police and subsequently through the courts has had 'its validity tested' (Leuprecht and Hall 2014, p. 95). However, researchers have gathered data from a wide variety of sources, not all of which assess the reliability and validity of the data as the courts do. According to Bright et al. (2012), the sources of data used by researchers applying SNA to criminal networks can be divided into five categories: offender databases, transcripts of physical or electronic surveillance, written summaries of police interrogations, transcripts of court proceedings, and online and print media. In addition to these sources, researchers have also used data from archival interviews (Athey and Bouchard 2013), non-government organisations (Everton and Cunningham 2012), interviews with former investigators (Koschade 2007) and think tanks (Leuprecht and Hall 2013). While all studies would benefit from using a reliability and validity weighting, it is strongly recommended that those that use these additional data sources with online and print media incorporate weightings similar to those used by law enforcement to reduce instances of incorrect data infiltrating the analysis.

Inconsistencies

A further data challenge is the inconsistencies that can occur in criminal databases (Sanders et al. 2015; Xu and Chen 2005). Several of those interviewed identified inconsistent data as a key challenge when applying SNA. For example, one analyst explained that if information is inconsistently entered into their databases it essentially becomes lost:

> So, if you wanted to find out, you might want to find out a particular person who's got a specific tattoo. So, you can run a query [search] for a tattoo, but in order to find that tattoo, someone at some point would have had to

put in a form. […] But what you will find is that people or members, they don't put in that specific form, they will actually mention it in the dossier, which is the narrative of that particular offender. So okay, I'm trying to locate Joe Blow who could have, I don't know, a big tattoo on his head that says 'criminal', or something like that, and if I put in a query for males, 25–30, whatever, have got 'criminal' [as a tattoo]. It [the database] will never bring it back because it will be in the narrative or the dossier and then if you're going to try and search the dossier of every 25–30-year-old criminal in Victoria it will probably take six months. (Analyst No. 14)

Therefore, a situation can arise whereby analysts and detectives cannot 'see' certain information that may be relevant to their investigation. For analysts, the outcome is that there may be valuable relational data that they are not aware of and is subsequently not included in an SNA.

This issue relates to a broader point raised by many research participants concerning data standard: *what* is being stored and *how* it is being stored (Sheptycki 2004). Several analysts also noted that the data they receive from external groups, including public and private companies, is often inconsistent. Given that these are critical sources of data for law enforcement (Victoria Police 2014), this is an area that needs examination. One analyst discussed how there are inconsistencies in how long data is kept by certain private businesses:

How long information is kept is an issue, because if somebody doesn't hang onto data then obviously, you can't use it. Locally that's seen if there is surveillance footage from a 7/11 or a service station or a shopping centre, that's great stuff, you can use that sometimes. But you have to jump onto it straight away because they only keep that thing for two weeks, sometimes a month, sometimes a week, some places only keep it for a few days. If police haven't turned up in a few days to say hang on we need such and such, it gets written over. That just comes down to their finances. (Analyst No. 7)

Many analysts were also frustrated with the lack of consistency in the information they receive from certain industries, such as telecommunications. As one analyst explained:

What you're going to get from one telco [telecommunications] company is quite often different from the outputs you'll get from different ones and the amount of hoops you'll have to jump through to get that in the first place. It's always a balancing act of risk assessments of what you would really like to get, what's available and how difficult it is to get it. (Analyst No. 8)

In Australia, steps have been taken to address this issue with the *Telecommunications (Interception and Access) Amendment (Data Retention) Act 2015*, now requiring telecommunication providers to retain particular types of metadata for two years.[3] This law is designed to ensure that there is consistency in the telecommunications industry concerning what information is collected and how long it is held for.[4] The problem for law enforcement agencies is there are a number of other industries and potential sources of information, such as privately held CCTV footage, where no such laws exist. These other sources of relational data vary dramatically in their availability and consistency. This issue is compounded by the fact that even when analysts do have the information they require to conduct SNA, it can be an immense challenge to get that data into a usable format.

Data Transformation

Once analysts have collected the necessary relational data to conduct SNA, it will need to be converted into a usable format. A requirement of SNA is that actors are represented as nodes and that relationships are represented as ties (Xu and Chen 2005). However, many criminal databases, particularly older ones, were not designed to store data in a format

---

[3] Telecommunications metadata consists of information including caller identity as well as call time and place. It does not include the contents of a phone conversation. For internet activity, it includes the email address and when it was sent, but not the subject line of an email or its contents.

[4] It is important to note that there has been considerable debate surrounding this law and similar legislation from overseas due to privacy concerns (see Breyer 2005; Newell 2014). For example, in 2006 the European Union Parliament passed what has become known as the 'Data Retention Directive', requiring member countries to store telecommunications metadata for at least 6 months and for up to 24 months (Vainio and Miettinen 2015, p. 290). However, in 2014 the Court of European Justice ruled that the Directive was invalid, stating that it violated fundamental rights, namely a right to privacy (Vainio and Miettinen 2015).

that can easily be used in SNA. Analysts will often have to manually go through their databases, extract the data and then convert it. For example, evidence of a relationship between two individuals might be recorded within a criminal database simply as 'Actor A was observed meeting with Actor B'. This information must then be manually entered into an association matrix (see Chap. 2), which is often created using Microsoft Excel. Several analysts complained about the time-consuming and labour-intensive nature of this process. As one analyst explained:

> I need to spend the next day working out how this different source of information, how I can integrate this with the information I've already got in a meaningful way [...]. It really comes down to people with enough energy and skills to be able to do something but to not be put off that I have to spend the next eight hours manually manipulating spreadsheets to be able to get them in a form that I can input to a chart. [However,] we should not be at a point where we are [...] manually mapping networks [...], it should be far more automated in the way that we do it. That's the barrier that we at least have some control over, [...] but it's still only scratching the surface. (Analyst No. 8)

While it was certainly evident that the time-consuming and manual nature of converting the data into a usable format was an important consideration, it was not clear from research participants to which extent they simply choose not to use SNA because of these factors. Furthermore, the point made by this last analyst concerning the automation of the data transformation process, and more broadly the application of SNA, was only raised by the one individual. There has been some research into automating SNA. For example, Ball (2016) suggested that 'data mining' and 'text mining' techniques will be critical to this process. Data mining involves the use of various algorithms to identify patterns in very large datasets (Ye 2014). Text mining is the analysis of natural language text, including the extraction of specific information from datasets (Weiss et al. 2005). However, Ball (2016) also cautioned that a great deal of further research is needed before the automation of SNA can be realised, including the development of the algorithms necessary for the extraction of social network data from criminal databases and open sources. Overall, it is evident that not only does the challenge of data incompleteness remain an issue today, but also that data incorrectness and inconsistencies, as well as data transformation, can significantly impact on analysts' ability to use SNA effectively.

Fuzzy Boundaries

The third characteristic of criminal networks, fuzzy boundaries (also called boundary specification), refers to the difficulty in determining their boundaries; that is, which actors and, just as importantly, which relationships, are to be included in an analysis (Décary-Hétu and Dupont 2012; Kossinets 2006). Among researchers a common approach to this issue is to put in place some form of specification rule or criteria that outline clearly which actors and relationships are to be included in the analysis (Burcher and Whelan 2015; Koschade 2006; Sparrow 1991). However, research is yet to examine how intelligence analysts approach this issue. Only one analyst mentioned the use of a formal boundary-specification rule. As this analyst explained, they try to confine their analysis to a particular location, group membership or a period of time:

> I would recommend to confine the boundaries with very basic information in such a way that it has certain themes or certain locations or a group of people. Then, when conducting an analysis using SNA on a group of individuals, the results will be available for the investigator as well as the analyst to look at periodically. If six months after they find new connections between individuals already identified, then it takes another form. Ideally, it would be beneficial to confine it to one period of time. (Analyst No. 16)

Several studies (Dijkstra et al. 2014; Duijn et al. 2014, p. 13) suggested that by not using a boundary-specification rule (also called 'no boundary' intelligence gathering) analysts can avoid setting the net too close, whereby actors/relationships may be missed due to the arbitrariness of such rules. Inadvertently excluding important individuals from an analysis was a key consideration for several analysts. For example, one analyst explained that actors that appear on the edges of a network might be key players: 'you can't dismiss the one that's sitting on the periphery either, it's just that he might be just keeping his head down' (Analyst No. 6). By putting in place a boundary-specification rule the concern is that actors who are on the periphery might be excluded from the analysis. This may go some way towards explaining why research participants do not use these rules, although this area requires further research. This approach may be better suited to large-scale investigations where law enforcement are attempting to examine criminal networks in their entirety (or 'macro' level networks) (Duijn et al. 2014, p. 13). An example would be an investigation focusing on the entire commodity chain of a particular illicit drug in a city. The problem for law enforcement agencies is they do not have the resources for each investigation to be examining such networks in their entirety, and will often instead focus on the sub-groups of these networks (see Chap. 5). Furthermore, the investigative focus of individual units is often quite narrow (see Chap. 5), meaning they are restricted in their ability to examine criminal networks fully. This means there are going to be times when analysts should be looking to apply a formal boundary-specification rule. At the time, Sparrow (1991) suggested that there were no obvious criteria for including and excluding actors. Since then there has been some research exploring different boundary-specification rules (Laumann et al. 1992), but few researchers have discussed their applicability to criminal networks (Kossinets 2006; Morris and Deckro 2013). The remainder of this section seeks to provide an in-depth examination of the different boundary-specification rules with a particular focus on their suitability to criminal networks and their use within operational law enforcement environments.

In an influential study on this topic, Laumann et al. (1992) present two broad approaches to defining the boundary of a network: the 'realist' approach and the 'nominalist' approach. In the realist approach, a boundary is defined by those that make up the network. This involves the analyst assuming the vantage point of the targeted individuals, whereby an individual actor is only considered part of the network if most of the group consider them to be a part of that social entity. This is an appropriate option when examining formal institutions, such as a sports clubs or a university (Morris and Deckro 2013). The problem with this approach for law enforcement is that they are often dealing with highly informal networks whose boundaries are extremely fluid (Bakker et al. 2012). This issue is summarised by one analyst: 'it's an ongoing process to keep your information up to date about that organisation and its forever changing, people are moving around, different spots, who's leading, who's not leading, sometimes they splinter, and they do operate reasonably secretly' (Analyst No. 4). This issue is examined in greater detail later in the chapter. This approach also has a potential paradoxical problem in that an actor may consider himself/herself to be a part of the network when the majority of the other individuals do not (Morris and Deckro 2013). An example of this can be found in youth gangs where it is common for individuals to claim membership in order to obtain some form of social status (White 2002), even in instances where they are not, in fact, a member. One analyst had experience with this type of 'big noting': 'we used to get a lot of people in the Asian field saying we're part of this particular gang and we used to find they were big noting themselves to earn a little bit of cred [credibility] in their community' (Analyst No. 21). This approach is likely to be challenging for analysts to apply, without the availability of very reliable informants to clearly establish legitimate members of the targeted network. For intelligence analysts, the application of the realist approach should not be ruled out altogether but is unlikely to be the most appropriate option for determining which actors to include.

The nominalist approach involves the analyst putting in place a conceptual framework that is designed to serve his/her own analytical objectives (Laumann et al. 1992). There are three 'definitional foci' used to define the boundaries of actor inclusion: actors, relations and activities (Laumann et al. 1992). It is critical that analysts make it clear which definitional foci they choose to use, as certain analytical findings will be directly impacted by this choice. For example, it will be no great surprise to find a network that was constructed using snowball sampling is a well-connected network (Laumann et al. 1992; Tsvetovat and Carley 2006). The first definitional focus, *actors*, involves the boundary of a network being set by the individual attributes or characteristics of the actors. Under this definitional focus, there are two sub-categories, the 'positional' approach and the 'reputational' approach. The positional approach involves the presence or absence of some attribute that designates a position within a group, such as formal membership. The problem with this approach for criminal networks is that membership is highly ambiguous and few groups, outside of the likes of outlaw motorcycle gangs through the use of gang patches, actively promote their membership (Burcher and Whelan 2015; Malm et al. 2011). This issue was raised by several interviewees:

> The clothing and the patches that would appear on that clothing would symbolise that person's membership and also their rank and particular roles within that group [...]. In the wider criminal view, those sorts of rigid arrangements are not so common. (Analyst No. 18)

> OMCG's [outlaw motorcycle gangs] tend to get a lot of attention because they are easily identifiable, understandable thing, you know, look there's an organised motorcycle gang. We can see them because they're riding big bikes and have patches which tell you which gang they are a part of. But them aside, most organised crime does not fit into a definable group. (Analyst No. 2)

Therefore, outside of the likes of outlaw motorcycle gangs this approach is unlikely to be appropriate for law enforcement. In contrast, the reputational approach 'utilizes the judgements of knowledgeable informants in delimiting participant actors' (Laumann et al. 1992, p. 67). While this approach is likely to be used by law enforcement, at times, it also relies heavily on the reliability and accuracy of the informants used (Coles 2001). The positional approach and the reputational approach can at times be used in combination.

The second definitional focus under the nominalist approach, *relations*, involves the analyst defining the boundary of a network based on individuals that have a relationship of a specific type, such as frequency of interaction. For example, two actors may only be included in the analysis if the frequency of their interaction surpasses a certain threshold, such as at least one phone call per week. This approach will often involve the use of snowball sampling, which, as noted earlier, will often unsurprisingly result in a network that is well connected. McGloin and Kirk

(2010) also highlight that when applying snowball sampling the analyst will at some point have to stop. As several analysts noted, however, choosing when to stop can be challenging:

> I walked in towards the tail end of an operation which had been running for a year and they had access to [Analyst] Notebook at that stage and they had this absolutely enormous print out that was meters long and a good metre high [...]. It just had hundreds of entities, persons, cars, phones, addresses, businesses and they had started an operation looking at a couple of offenders [...]. What they hadn't done at the start of the operation, they hadn't clearly identified the scope of how far they would go, who would they look at, what offences, would they look at individuals directly related to or indirectly related by however many degrees of association. So, parameters for the investigation hadn't been firmly set or if they had the guys had forgotten about them. (Analyst No. 7)

> I've seen linked charts that have gone for 10–15 meters in length, big A1 (piece of paper) on a plotter of just who's friends with who and it just keeps going, and going, and going, and there just doesn't seem to be an end to it. (Analyst No. 1)

This gives some indication as to how easily it is for the boundaries of an investigation to blow out. A final problem of using the nominalist approach and the definitional focus of relations is that it relies on the ability of the analyst to determine the type of relationship that any two actors may have, and as almost all of those interviewed mentioned, doing this in practice can be extremely difficult:

> One of the tricky parts is trying to identify who is and who isn't a part of that network or that group of offending. You can come across people who might be together but are they just mates or are they co-offenders or are they both and how do you understand that? [...] Who is part of this criminal network and who isn't, and trying to pick those two apart is tricky and time-consuming. (Analyst No. 2)

> Determining who is not relevant to the criminal enterprise, because people will be connected to vast networks and not all those connections are in context to criminal activity, even if they are a known criminal actor. Making

sure those relationships are understood with some degree of clarity means you can't discount some people as being part of a network as much as you can count people in. (Analyst No. 5)

As these analysts suggest, it may not just be case of determining the type of relationship that any two actors have, but identifying multiple relationship types. For example, it is not inconceivable for it to be equally appropriate to define two actors by their friendship, kinship or co-offending relationship (Duijn and Klerks 2014; Kenney 2007). This also supports the point made in Chap. 4 that, where possible, researchers and practitioners should incorporate link weights. Despite these challenges, if law enforcement agencies can gather sufficient information about the relationships in a network, this approach to boundary specification would be suitable for criminal networks.

The final definitional focus involves the boundary being set by an activity or event (Laumann et al. 1992). For example, actors may be considered part of a network if they are involved in a specific event (such as a terrorist attack) or a specific activity (such as the distribution of a particular drug). Again, this is an approach likely to be used by law enforcement, and it has certainly been used by researchers looking at specific terrorist attacks (Azad and Gupta 2011; Burcher and Whelan 2015; Koschade 2006; Krebs 2002; Rodriguez 2005). However, Kossinets (2006) argued that this approach is problematic: as attendance at a particular event is self-selective, certain individuals in a network may not be at this event for a number of reasons. For example, it is not unrealistic to assume that at times higher-ranking members of a criminal network will have subordinates take their place at particular events. By focusing on just one event there is the possibility that not all members of the network will be included in the analysis. On the other hand, this approach can overcome the challenge of determining the formal membership of a criminal network, making this a useful approach for law enforcement. Finally, it should be noted that it is possible to use more than one definitional focus to determine the inclusion of actors. While none of the approaches to defining the boundary of a network should be ruled out by law enforcement entirely, it is recommended that analysts predominantly use the nominalist approach and the use of either relation or activity definitional focus as they are the most appropriate for criminal networks. Each approach has limitations and it is critical that analysts are aware of these and how they may impact any findings. Importantly, the choice of boundary specification should not be random, but a theoretically informed decision based on the type of network being targeted and the objectives of the investigation.

Dynamic

The final characteristic of criminal networks refers to the dynamic nature of social networks. The relationship between any two individuals, including the presence or absence of a connection and the relative strength of that relationship, is in a constant state of flux (Burcher and Whelan 2017; Lauchs et al. 2011). The challenges associated with the dynamic nature of criminal networks were something all analysts were well aware of, as one summarised:

> When we look into networks in a law enforcement environment we generally look at them over a certain snap shot in time, like a time and place. We may not get to know everything about that network until years down the track when we might investigate them from another angle or another agency investigates them from another angle. So, when we do any analysis it's got to be, it comes with lot of caveats as to this is not the entire picture, this is what we believe is happening at this point in time and it's just a matter of later on down the track we might realise what we were actually looking at but it's just the nature of the beast. (Analyst No. 21)

Because any SNA is only a snapshot of that network at one point in time, any findings may soon be out of date. The problem for law enforcement is keeping their databases up to date with the necessary relational data to conduct SNA. Several analysts noted that this is not an easy task:

> I'm finding out in the real world with these criminals their life changes much faster than what our records do […], so that's a huge limitation […].

They come and go, they use each other for business or pleasure as they feel fit and [are] quite happy to turf them and move on and we just don't have the resources [to monitor those changes]. We're not concentrating on particular people, you just can't do that all the time. Their friendship groups change so quickly whereas those maps don't. If you relied on the intelligence that's there, that's been pulled in, it's going to be old, so really, I would say that's the biggest limitation. (Analyst No. 9)

We do regularly update our profiles on the individuals in the group. So, we're constantly going back and checking to see if there are any new players or if they have joined up to any new businesses or new property or new cars. Just continually updating who they are and everything about them and trying to keep track of their practices. [...] It is difficult because at our level they tend to be quite good at avoiding attention, so it can be quite difficult, they often don't come to the attention of police often. It does get difficult to see changes and a lot of it does come down to surveillance, if they are a current target, so a lot of it needs to be done by the investigators [...]. So, it is difficult, it is resource intensive. [...] It's usually just a group of associates who mix, come together, usually the core group remains constant but it can vary in terms of its structure and participants. [...] Just who comes and who goes, someone might get locked up, someone might lose trust of the group or they might meet somebody else and bring somebody else on board with a different expertise. (Analyst No. 25)

This is a critical point of difference between the type of retrospective analysis that has been dominating the SNA literature (Everton and Cunningham 2012; Harris-Hogan 2012; Mullins and Dolnik 2010; Natarajan 2006) and trying to apply SNA in 'real-time', where it is a constant battle for law enforcement agencies to keep their knowledge up to date. Sanders et al. (2015, p. 721) note: 'although technologies have been installed to assist in capturing and coding real-time data, the situational pace of policing can make this challenging'. This is also an important finding as it goes against one of the few studies that have examined SNA in an operational environment, Johnson and Reitzal (2011, p. 5), who suggested that 'a near real-time social map of the network of a targeted group' that is reflective of the 'on the ground' reality can '*easily*' [emphasis added] be provided to officers. In contrast, Duijn and Klerks'

(2014, p. 153) study exploring the use of SNA by Dutch law enforcement agencies found that they were using SNA in 'real-time', but to achieve this they had to combine 'multiple data sources into one relational database'. Duijn and Klerks (2014, p. 153) note that although bringing together data from multiple sources is part of everyday police work, 'continuously and structurally combining multiple sources [...] aimed at identifying criminal networks' is not. One analyst interviewed had reached a similar conclusion, suggesting that in order to better monitor the changes that occur in criminal networks their organisation would need a similar relational database, or as they put it, an 'active library':

> A recent project, well it's an active project looking at forensic intelligence linking methodology, and part of the recommendations to the development team [for that project] were to suggest that we have an active library using SNA [...]. We look at crime trends but we don't really look at our hierarchical groups to see the changes in them. I envision a dynamic active library where you could look every month to assess incarcerations, who's moved up, who's moved down, who's been taken out of the scene. But as an organisation, we don't really look at that in-depth and I think we should be, it's a key element in probably keeping tabs on crime. (Analyst No. 11)

This would suggest that any law enforcement agencies that are looking to more closely monitor the dynamics of criminal networks will require an 'active library' in which relational data about the targeted network is pooled together from multiple sources and regularly updated. Actually maintaining an active library, however, will be extremely challenging given the rate at which criminal networks change. While their dynamic nature is certainly acknowledged in the broader literature (see Chap. 2), interviewees identified that there has been insufficient attention to just how quickly such groups change. For example, several analysts discussed how criminal networks will regularly change who they offend with:

> With a lot of the problems we've had out in this region, there's an awful lot of people involved and they chop and change their groups and who they're offending with. When it's like that it's very tough to stay on top of and they're well-schooled in police methodologies and they share that informa-

tion and that information is spread and it's quite difficult to stay on top of them. (Analyst No. 6)

They'll come together for a short period of time, accomplish what they want to accomplish in that period of time, which we're talking 6–12 months at most and then all go their separate ways and then two will go over here, they just move around so much. (Analyst No. 8)

Previous studies that have looked at the changes that occur in criminal networks have often involved large periods of time between each analysis. For example, Bright and Delaney's (2013) examination of a drug-trafficking network over 8 years was divided into four two-year periods, Helfstein and Wright's (2011) examination of several terrorist networks over 5 years was divided into five one-year periods, and McCuish et al.'s (2014) examination of a homicide co-offenders gang over 20 years was divided into four five-year periods. While the availability of suitable data will have a disproportionate influence on the time periods applied, the responses of research participants would suggest that important changes in criminal networks happen quite frequently and may go undetected when applying SNA so infrequently. This suggests that both researchers and analysts would benefit from applying SNA at more frequent intervals, such as monthly (see Everton and Cunningham 2012), when conducting longitudinal analyses of criminal networks. This point is reinforced by several analysts who suggested that criminal networks are becoming even more dynamic. They believed that one of the driving factors behind this change was a willingness among the criminal fraternity to prioritise monetary gain over other concerns, such as past grievances or ethnic divides. As several analysts explained:

So, it's very fluid at the moment and that's what we're seeing and we do see old networks crop up regularly and we recognise a lot of those names but we also see new names crop up and people we didn't think would associate or do business together, might have had conflict in the past, but for the sake of money and business we will do business again. (Analyst No. 21)

[It's] like project management for really big business now, or project management on a building site. You get subbies [sub-contractors] to do different parts of the job and you'll have Lebanese gentlemen will import the heroin or the crystal meth or whatever and then he will find a Chinese cook or he will find a cook that's a local that he knows will do the job correctly and they sub contract out their work. So, multiculturalism works really well in this respect, there are some areas where organised crime looks like it's a family concern but it really isn't, its very much become a shadow of big business. (Analyst No. 19)

This would in part help to explain the difficulty law enforcement are having with trying to keep their databases up to date. Compounding this are changes in technology which may allow social connections to appear to be highly transitory in nature, or at least in the eyes of law enforcement. For example, with the rise of IM and VoIP (Voice over internet protocol allows for voice communication over the internet), there is less of a need for criminal groups to meet face-to-face or to make phone calls. As several analysts explained:

You might do your business by communicating on your PlayStation 2 games and using VoIP and those things that authorities don't have access to. Very canny criminals will do that. (Analyst No. 19)

There's one thing that we have noticed, it's to do with technology once again. These days' people tend to communicate through texts or Snapchat or Facebook, they are really hard to trace the way people communicate. [It] used to be a phone call and then you would do traces you know and drop that in to, do a network analysis through that. These days it's much, much harder, that's the change—the change is through technology. (Analyst No. 3)

The monitoring of face-to-face meetings and phone calls are both traditional intelligence gathering avenues for law enforcement. However, as a result of this technology allowing offenders to instantly communicate with one another securely, criminal groups may appear less connected than they were in the past. According to several analysts, this issue is only likely to grow for law enforcement agencies:

The landscape is changing and it's changing dramatically and our traditional methods need to be refocused and what we rely on heavily now will be very different in 10 years' time. It's the challenge of keeping up with that and keeping skilled up in that. So, it's really up skilling more into a cyber sphere, less of phones. We're still going to use traditional methods in many ways, like the investigators will still have their sources and their surveillance and all that, that's going to be relevant. But are phones going to be relevant given how much people have shifted from actual phone conversations to text messaging, to using apps to communicate via games. There's a range of ways in which people in general are communicating and criminals are no different, its keeping up with that challenge and educated on what we should look for and how we overcome that. (Analyst No. 21)

[The] Australian Crime Commission (renamed the Australian Criminal Intelligence Commission or ACIC) have put out, they've said within five years TI (telecommunications interception) will be irrelevant because people don't talk on mobile phone to mobile phone. It's the use of these encrypted networks like your WhatsApp, your Viber, even Facebook and all that. They're 10 years ahead of the technology that we use here.[5] (Analyst No. 24)

The implications for law enforcement are that, in time, current sources of relational data may vanish entirely. The implications for contemporary law enforcement are that there is a greater chance that the data they use is or soon will be out of date. Again, this reinforces the notion that while an active library would be desirable in order to monitor the dynamic changes that occur in criminal networks, implementing this in practice would be immensely challenging.

---

[5] In 2018, the Australian Government passed the Telecommunications and Other Legislation Amendment (Assistance and Access) Act 2018 which requires industry (such as Apple and Google) to allow law enforcement access to encrypted devices. However, even before these new powers were introduced, it was suggested that criminals will simply move on to other forms of communication, such as through the dark web (Glance 2017). Furthermore, it has been suggested that implementing such legislation in practice may not be technologically possible. For example, former head of the US National Security Agency (NSA), Chris Inglis, stated: 'I don't know how feasible it is to achieve the kind of access the Government might want to have under the rule of law, the technology is tough to get exactly right' (Belot 2017).

Conclusion

The primary finding of this chapter is that the characteristics of criminal networks heavily impact on the ability of intelligence analysts to apply SNA in operational environments. While the software packages available to analysts have improved markedly, the pace of their development has been surpassed by the amount of data now being collected and stored by law enforcement. This places limits of the size of the networks analysts can examine. Alongside incompleteness, it was clear from research participants and the literature (Morris and Deckro 2013; Xu and Chen 2005) that there are several other 'data challenges', including incorrectness, inconsistency and data transformation, that can equally impact on analysts ability to use SNA effectively. It was evident from the interviews that researchers may benefit from using a reliability and validity weighting when applying SNA, and in doing so reduce the chances of incorrect data entering their analysis. The chapter provided the first in-depth examination of boundary-specification rules and their appropriateness for use by intelligence analysts. It was concluded that although no boundary-specification rule should be deemed inapplicable to criminal networks, the most appropriate for law enforcement would be the nominalist approach with the use of either relation or activity focus. Finally, the chapter examined the dynamic nature of social networks, finding that law enforcement agencies wanting to better understand the changes that occur in criminal networks should develop an 'active library' where relational data from multiple sources is regularly pulled together and converted into a usable format in one database. It was determined, however, that the rate of change that occurs within criminal networks is incredibly fast, and maintaining an active library would prove immensely challenging. To further understanding of the challenges of applying SNA to criminal networks, the next three chapters examine what has been labelled the 'organisational characteristics of law enforcement agencies' (Burcher and Whelan 2017, p. 1).

References

B. Akhgar, G.B. Saathoff, H.R. Arabnia, R. Hill, A. Staniforth, P.S. Bayerl, *Application of big data for national security: a practitioner's guide to emerging technologies* (Elsevier, Oxford, 2015)

N.C. Athey, M. Bouchard, The BALCO scandal: the social structure of a steroid distribution network. Global Crime **14**(2–3), 216–237 (2013)

S. Azad, A. Gupta, A quantitative assessment on 26/11 Mumbai attack using social network analysis. J. Terrorism Res. **2**(2), 4–14 (2011)

R.M. Bakker, J. Raab, H.B. Milward, A preliminary theory of dark network resilience. J. Policy Anal. Manage. **31**(1), 33–62 (2012)

L. Ball, Automating social network analysis: a power tool for counter-terrorism. Secur. J. **29**(2), 147–168 (2016)

H. Belot, Ex-NSA boss questions encrypted message access laws proposed by Malcolm Turnbull, *Australian Broadcasting Corporation* (2017). http://www.abc.net.au/news/2017-08-01/former-nsa-boss-questions-malcolm-turnbull-encryption-laws/8761542. Accessed 4 July 2020

G. Berlusconi, Do all the pieces matter? assessing the reliability of law enforcement data sources for the network analysis of wire taps. Global Crime **14**(1), 61–81 (2013)

G. Bichler, S. Lim, E. Larin, Tactical social network analysis: using affiliation networks to aid serial homicide investigation. Homicide Stud. **21**(2), 133–158 (2016)

P. Breyer, Telecommunications data retention and human rights: the compatibility of blanket traffic data retention with the ECHR. Eur. Law J. **11**(3), 365–375 (2005)

D.A. Bright, Disrupting and dismantling dark networks: lessons from social network analysis and law enforcement simulations, in *Illuminating dark networks: the study of clandestine groups and organisations*, ed. by L. M. Gerdes, (Cambridge University Press, New York, 2015), pp. 39–51

D.A. Bright, Using social network analysis to design crime prevention strategies: a case study of methamphetamine manufacture and trafficking, in *Crime prevention in the 21st century: insightful approaches for crime prevention initiatives*, ed. by B. LeClerc, E. U. Savona, (Springer International Publishing, Switzerland, 2017), pp. 143–164

D.A. Bright, J.J. Delaney, Evolution of a drug trafficking network: mapping changes in network structure and function across time. Global Crime **14**(2–3), 238–260 (2013)

D.A. Bright, C. Greenhill, M. Reynolds, A. Ritter, C. Morselli, The use of actor-level attributes and centrality measures to identify key actors: a case study of an Australian drug trafficking network. J. Contemp. Crim. Justice **31**(3), 262–278 (2015a)

D.A. Bright, C. Greenhill, A. Ritter, C. Morselli, Networks within networks: using multiple link types to examine network structure and identify key actors in a drug trafficking operation. Global Crime **16**(3), 1–19 (2015b)

D.A. Bright, C.E. Hughes, J. Chalmers, Illuminating dark networks: a social network analysis of an Australian drug trafficking syndicate. Crime Law Soc. Chang. **57**(2), 151–176 (2012)

J.-P. Brodeur, B. Dupont, Knowledge workers or "knowledge" workers? Polic. Soc. **16**(1), 7–26 (2006)

M. Burcher, C. Whelan, Social network analysis and small group 'dark' networks: an analysis of the London bombers and the problem of 'fuzzy' boundaries. Global Crime **16**(2), 104–122 (2015)

M. Burcher, C. Whelan, Social network analysis as a tool for criminal intelligence: understanding its potential from the perspectives of intelligence analysts. Trends Org. Crime **21**(3), 278–294 (2017)

D.L. Carter, *Law enforcement intelligence: a guide for state, local, and tribal law enforcement agencies* (2009), No. 24 July 2012. https://it.ojp.gov/documents/d/e050919201-IntelGuide_web.pdf. Accessed 21 August 2018

Y. Charette, A.V. Papachristos, The network dynamics of co-offending careers, *Social Networks* (2017). http://www.sciencedirect.com/science/article/pii/S0378873316302234. Accessed 25 May 2017

N. Coles, It's not what you know it's who you know: analysing serious crime groups as social networks. Br. J. Criminol. **41**(4), 580–594 (2001)

A.F. Colladon, E. Remondi, Using social network analysis to prevent money laundering. Expert Syst. Appl. **67**, 49–58 (2017)

D. Décary-Hétu, B. Dupont, The social network of hackers. Global Crime **13**(3), 160–175 (2012)

L.J. Dijkstra, A.V. Yakushev, P.A.C. Duijn, A.V. Boukhanovsky, P.M.A. Sloot, Inference of the Russian drug community from one of the largest social networks in the Russian Federation. Qual. Quant. **48**(5), 2739–2755 (2014)

P.A.C. Duijn, V. Kashirin, P.M.A. Sloot, The relative ineffectiveness of criminal network disruption. Sci. Rep. **4**(4238), 1–15 (2014)

P.A.C. Duijn, P.P.H.M. Klerks, Social network analysis applied to criminal networks: recent developments in Dutch law enforcement, in *Networks and network analysis for defence and security*, ed. by A. J. Masys, (Springer, Heidelberg, 2014), pp. 121–159

P.A.C. Duijn, P.M.A. Sloot, From data to disruption. Digit. Investig. **15**, 39–45 (2015)

S.F. Everton, D. Cunningham, Detecting significant changes in dark networks. Behav. Sci. Terrorism Polit. Aggression **5**(2), 1–21 (2012)

S.F. Everton, D. Cunningham, Dark network resilience in a hostile environment: optimizing centralization and density. Criminol. Criminal Justice Law Soc. **16**(1), 1–20 (2015)

O. Frank, Sampling and estimation in large social networks. Soc. Networks **1**(1), 91–101 (1978)

D. Glance, Australia's planned decryption law would weaken cybersecurity. *The Conversation* (2017). http://theconversation.com/australias-planned-decryption-law-would-weaken-cybersecurity-81028. Accessed 31 July 2017

D. Gunnell, J. Hillier, L. Blakeborough, *Social network analysis of an urban street gang using police intelligence data* (2016). https://www.gov.uk/government/uploads/system/uploads/attachment_data/file/491578/horr89.pdf. Accessed 22 April 2016

S. Harris-Hogan, Anatomy of a terrorist cell: a study of the network uncovered in Sydney in 2005. Behav. Sci. Terrorism Polit. Aggression **5**(2), 1–18 (2012)

S. Helfstein, D. Wright, Covert or convenient? evolution of terror attack networks. J. Confl. Resolut. **55**(5), 785–813 (2011)

D.C. Hofmann, O. Gallupe, Leadership protection in drug-trafficking networks. Global Crime **16**(2), 123–138 (2015)

C.E. Hutchins, M. Benham-Hutchins, Hiding in plain sight: criminal network analysis. Comput. Math. Org. Theor. **16**(1), 89–111 (2010)

IBM, *IBM big data success stories* (IBM, 2011). http://public.dhe.ibm.com/software/data/sw-library/big-data/ibm-big-data-success.pdf. Accessed 3 June 2017

E.E. Joh, Policing by numbers: big data and the fourth amendment. Wash. Law Rev. **89**(1), 35–68 (2014)

J.A. Johnson, J.D. Reitzal, *Social network analysis in an operational environment: defining the utility of a network approach for crime analysis using the Richmond City Police Department as a case study* (2011). http://www.coginta.org/en/document/policy_working_paper_series?page=3. Accessed 8 August 2012

M. Kenney, The architecture of drug trafficking: network forms of organisation in the Colombian cocaine trade. Global Crime **8**(3), 233–259 (2007)

S. Koschade, A social network analysis of Jemaah Islamiyah: the applications to counterterrorism and intelligence. Stud. Conflict Terrorism **29**(6), 559–575 (2006)

S. Koschade, *The internal dynamics of terrorist cells: a social network analysis of terrorist cells in an Australian context*, PhD thesis, Queensland University of Technology, 2007

G. Kossinets, Effects of missing data in social networks. Soc. Networks **28**(3), 247–268 (2006)

V. Krebs, Mapping networks of terrorist cells. Connections **24**(3), 43–52 (2002)

A. Kriegler, Using social network analysis to profile organised crime. Inst. Secur. Stud. **57**, 1–8 (2014)

M. Lauchs, R. Keast, N. Yousefpour, Corrupt police networks: uncovering hidden relationship patterns, functions and roles. Polic. Soc. **21**(1), 110–127 (2011)

E.O. Laumann, P.V. Marsden, D. Prensky, *Research methods in social network analysis* (Transaction Publishers, New Brunswick, NJ, 1992)

C. Leuprecht, K. Hall, Networks as strategic repertoires: functional differentiation among Al-Shabaab terror cells. Global Crime **14**(2–3), 287–310 (2013)

C. Leuprecht, K. Hall, Why terror networks are dissimilar: how structure relates to function, in *Networks and network analysis for defence and security*, ed. by A. J. Masys, (Springer International Publishing, Cham, 2014), pp. 83–120

A. Malm, G. Bichler, Networks of collaborating criminals: assessing the structural vulnerability of drug markets. J. Res. Crime Delinq. **48**(2), 271–297 (2011)

A. Malm, G. Bichler, R. Nash, Co-offending between criminal enterprise groups. Global Crime **12**(2), 112–128 (2011)

A. Malm, G. Bichler, S. Van De Walle, Comparing the ties that bind criminal networks: is blood thicker than water? Secur. J. **23**(1), 52–74 (2010)

A. Malm, J.B. Kinney, N.R. Pollard, Social network and distance correlates of criminal associates involved in illicit drug production. Secur. J. **21**(1–2), 77–94 (2008)

E.C. McCuish, M. Bouchard, R.R. Corrado, The search for suitable homicide co-offenders among gang members. J. Contemp. Crim. Justice **31**(3), 319–336 (2014)

J.M. McGloin, D.S. Kirk, An overview of social network analysis. J. Criminal Justice Educ. **21**(2), 169–181 (2010)

R.M. Medina, Social network analysis: a case study of the Islamist terrorist network. Secur. J. **27**(1), 97–121 (2014)

J.F. Morris, R.F. Deckro, SNA data difficulties with dark networks. Behav. Sci. Terrorism Polit. Aggression **5**(2), 70–93 (2013)

C. Morselli, J. Roy, Brokerage qualifications in ringing operations. Criminology **46**(1), 71–98 (2008)

T. Mullane, *NSW Police Force crime prevention strategy 2015–2017* (New South Wales Police Force, 2015). http://www.police.nsw.gov.au/__data/assets/pdf_file/0019/392131/Crime_Prevention_Strategy_2015-2017_Online.pdf. Accessed 20 September 2016

S. Mullins, A. Dolnik, An exploratory, dynamic application of social network analysis for modelling the development of Islamist terror cells in the West. Behav. Sci. Terrorism Polit. Aggression **2**(1), 3–29 (2010)

M. Natarajan, Understanding the structure of a large heroin distribution network: a quantitative analysis of qualitative data. J. Quant. Criminol. **22**(2), 171–192 (2006)

NCIS, *The National Intelligence Model* (NCIS, 2000). http://www.intelligence-analysis.net/National%20Intelligence%20Model.pdf. Accessed 12 July 2012

B.C. Newell, Law enforcement jumps on the big data bandwagon: automated license plate recognition systems, information privacy, and access to government information. Maine Law Rev. **66**(2), 397–436 (2014)

J. Ratcliffe, Intelligence-led policing and the problems of turning rhetoric into practice. Polic. Soc. **12**(1), 53–66 (2002)

J. Ratcliffe, Crime mapping and the training needs of law enforcement. Eur. J. Crim. Policy Res. **10**(1), 65–83 (2004)

J. Ratcliffe, J. Sheptycki, Setting the strategic agenda, in *Strategic thinking in criminal intelligence*, ed. by J. Ratcliffe, (Federation Press, Sydney, 2004), pp. 248–268

N. Roberts, S.F. Everton, Strategies for combating dark networks. J. Soc. Struct. **12**(2), 1–32 (2011)

J.A. Rodriguez, The March 11th terrorist network: in its weakness lies its strength, *CiteSeer* (2005). http://citeseerx.ist.psu.edu/viewdoc/summary?doi=10.1.1.98.4408. Accessed 7 August 2012

F. Saidi, Z. Trabelsi, K. Salah, H.B. Ghezala, Approaches to analyze cyber terrorist communities: survey and challenges. Comput. Secur. **66**, 66–80 (2017)

C.B. Sanders, C. Weston, N. Schott, Police innovations, 'secret squirrels' and accountability: empirically studying intelligence-led policing in Canada. Br. J. Criminol. **55**(4), 711–729 (2015)

J. Sheptycki, Editorial reflections on surveillance and intelligence-led policing. Polic. Soc. **9**(4), 311–314 (2000)

J. Sheptycki, Organizational pathologies in police intelligence systems: some contributions to the lexicon of intelligence-led policing. Eur. J. Criminol. **1**(3), 307–332 (2004)

J. Sheptycki, The police intelligence division-of-labour. Int. J. Res. Policy **27**(6), 620–635 (2017)

T. Spapens, Interaction between criminal groups and law enforcement: the case of ecstasy in the Netherlands. Global Crime **12**(1), 19–40 (2011)

M.K. Sparrow, The application of network analysis to criminal intelligence: an assessment of the prospects. Soc. Networks **13**(3), 251–274 (1991)

S.J. Strang, Network analysis in criminal intelligence, in *Networks and network analysis for defence and security*, ed. by A. J. Masys, (Springer International Publishing, Cham, 2014), pp. 1–26

M.A. Tayebi, U. Glasser, *Social network analysis in predictive policing: concepts, models and methods* (Springer International Publishing, Switzerland, 2016)

M. Tsvetovat, K.M. Carley, On effectiveness of wiretap programs in mapping social networks. Comput. Math. Org. Theor. **13**(1), 63–87 (2006)

N. Vainio, S. Miettinen, Telecommunications data retention after Digital Rights Ireland: legislative and judicial reactions in the member states. Int. J. Law Inf. Technol. **23**(3), 290–309 (2015)

R. van der Hulst, Introduction to social network analysis (SNA) as an investigative tool. Trends Org. Crime **12**(2), 101–121 (2009)

F. Varese, The structure and the content of criminal connections: the Russian mafia in Italy. Eur. Sociol. Rev. **29**(5), 899–909 (2013)

Victoria Police, *Victoria Police blue paper: a vision for Victoria Police 2025* (Victoria Police, 2014). http://www.police.vic.gov.au/content.asp?Document_ID=42063. Accessed 14 December 2016

S.M. Weiss, N. Indurkhya, T. Zhang, F.J. Damerau, *Text mining: predictive methods for analyzing unstructured information* (Springer, New York, 2005)

R. White, Understanding youth gangs. Trends Issues Crime Crim. Justice **237**, 1–6 (2002)

J. Xu, H. Chen, Criminal network analysis and visualization. Commun. ACM **48**(6), 100–107 (2005)

N. Ye, *Data mining: theories, algorithms, and examples* (CRC Press, Boca Raton, 2014)

J. Yuan, J. Cao, B. Xia, Arresting strategy based on dynamic criminal networks changing over time. Discret. Dyn. Nat. Soc. **2013**, 1–9 (2013)

5

Social Network Analysis and the Organisational Characteristics of Law Enforcement Agencies: Investigative Focus

Introduction

The organisational environment in which intelligence analysts operate and the unique aspects of these settings have the potential to impact on the extent to which intelligence analysts can apply social network analysis (SNA). The organisational characteristics of law enforcement agencies are divided into three broad categories: *Investigative Focus*; *Working Relationships*; and *IT Software, Systems and Training*. The next three chapters aim to advance understanding of SNA as an investigative tool for crime intelligence by being the first to examine these organisational characteristics as a whole. While each of the characteristics, such as the working relationships between analysts and managers, is a concern for intelligence analysts more broadly (Ratcliffe 2005), these chapters are only interested in how they relate to the use of SNA. While the generalisability of the findings in each chapter is limited due to the small number of law enforcement agencies involved, each of these characteristics, such as the challenges associated with IT software, systems and training, is likely to be found in varying degrees in almost all police organisations (Chen et al. 2003; Sheptycki 2004). These chapters will analyse each of

© The Author(s) 2020   **131**
M. Burcher, *Social Network Analysis and Law Enforcement*, Crime Prevention and
Security Management, https://doi.org/10.1007/978-3-030-47771-4_5

the organisational characteristics of law enforcement agencies in relation to how they may impact on an analyst's ability to use SNA, beginning with *Investigative Focus*. Investigative focus refers to how the objectives and priorities of an investigation, and more broadly that of the unit/taskforce that analysts are embedded in, impact on how SNA is used and the opportunities analysts have to apply it. Investigative focus concerns the 'size' of the network being targeted, the emphasis within law enforcement agencies on facilitating the prosecution of offenders and whether the investigation is predominantly reactive or proactive in nature.

Investigation Size

Several analysts suggested that the size of an investigation is one of the key factors in determining whether or not they use SNA. In this instance, size does not refer to the number of detectives/analysts involved or the amount of resources being utilised; it simply refers to the number of individuals being targeted (persons of interest) in an investigation. Consistent with network analysis literature (Mullins 2012; Perliger and Pedahzur 2011; Scott and Carrington 2011), many interviewees felt that SNA was best utilised on 'large' networks. As noted in Chap. 2, there is little consensus around what constitutes a large network. Several interviewees had a slightly different idea as to what it is, suggesting that it is a network of approximately 50 or more actors. This is explained by one analyst:

> So, when looking at 50 or more people I've found the value of it was, yes, you do identify the key players that we already know a lot about anyway. And we have got a lot of information about them because we are repeatedly targeting them, but it really helps to highlight those peripheral players that we don't pick up on generally. (Analyst No. 22)

According to several analysts interviewed, however, they have limited opportunities to use SNA. This is because in their view the investigations they are involved in simply do not allow it due to the limited number of individuals being targeted (under 50 actors). This is best summarised by one analyst:

One of the difficulties I think in using statistical measures[1] is that often the networks that we are looking at, particularly in operational, day-to-day policing are quite small, under 50 people [...]. If you're looking at an international organisation that has thousands of members, then a statistical analysis will be more descriptive and probably give you more direction. (Analyst No. 5)

This analyst indicated that they have limited opportunities to apply SNA because in their view the groups they are investigating 'day-to-day' are too small to warrant its use. There would appear to be a disconnect between researchers and practitioners, and the size of the networks to which they apply SNA. While it is noted in Chap. 2 that some of the SNA literature suggests that it might be better utilised on larger networks, there are numerous examples of SNA providing insight into small networks (under 50 actors). By restricting the use of SNA to networks considered to be 'large', intelligence analysts may be missing an opportunity to develop further insight into small networks.

What compounds this issue, according to one analyst, is that on average the networks they are investigating are getting smaller: 'they're getting smaller, they're smaller cells but I suppose that's more the organised crime picture [...]. You're seeing more people operating by themselves or in very small cells, one to three people' (Analyst No. 24). Despite this point being raised only by one analyst, it supports the findings of previous research (discussed in Chap. 2) that criminal groups are looking to operate in smaller and more loosely connected networks (Arquilla 2014; Bright et al. 2012; Kenney 2007; Natarajan 2006).

Several analysts suggested that the size of an investigation is heavily influenced by the type of crime that it focuses on, which in turn can limit their opportunities to apply SNA. For example, there are certain crime types where offenders regularly offend on their own. For example, as one analyst explained, 'sex offenders, [...] they're not a group necessarily, they're not associated with each other' (Analyst No. 10). This is supported by research which has shown that sexual offenders, both male

---

[1] Statistical measures are a reference to the mathematical computations used in SNA, such as betweenness centrality (see Chap. 2).

(Ioannou et al. 2017) and female (Bourke et al. 2014), tend to act alone. There are of course exceptions to this, such as 'child sex rings' (Wild 1989, p. 553). Whereas other offences, such as the distribution of illicit drugs, will often require the involvement of numerous actors (Giommoni et al. 2016; Morselli 2009). As another analyst discussed, SNA provides insight into networks involved in such types of offending: 'I find it's all dependent on the crime type and depending on who you're looking at. But if you're working on a OMCG [outlaw motorcycle gang] group or a drug syndicate I think it's critical to know who's talking to who, where people fit, who's the middle man [...]. It [SNA] shows you what the criminal picture is' (Analyst No. 24).

It has also been well documented that law enforcement personnel are regularly rotated within their organisation and placed on different 'jobs', investigating different crime types (Sanders et al. 2015; Taylor and Russell 2012; Wood 1997). Therefore, according to one analyst, depending on the type of crime that they are investigating or the job they are involved with, they can go many months without applying SNA: 'the times that I use it [SNA], practice it, has gone against me because of time and the jobs that I've been put on. [...] I don't normally touch it for months of the year, I wouldn't touch it' (Analyst No. 5). As this analyst suggests, a key impact of having limited opportunities to apply SNA is that their lack of regular practice means that they find it difficult to use when afforded the opportunity. While a lack of opportunities to practise would affect most analytical tasks undertaken by analysts, this issue is especially problematic for the more technical aspects of SNA, such as the use of link/attribute weightings. Given that many interviewees felt that SNA is best utilised on larger networks, the requirement that analysts be rotated may mean that the already limited opportunities to apply SNA become even more infrequent.

Prosecution-Oriented

The investigations that analysts are involved with are predominantly focused on the collection of evidence, charging suspects and subsequently developing a brief of evidence in order to help bring about the successful prosecution of offenders. This is summarised by one analyst: 'in the context of individual investigations, most of our investigations are traditional in that there is an objective to charge people with particular criminal offences and achieve criminal prosecutions in criminal courts' (Analyst No. 18). It was also noted by most interviewees that their role in an investigation tends primarily to involve the collection and analysis of information that supports the successful prosecution of offenders:

> Probably the largest proportion of our intelligence analyst's time is spent on assembling the information, analysing that information and presenting it in a fashion that can support those criminal prosecutions. (Analyst No. 18)

> So, it's providing that analytical support to basically, you know, the key objective of putting those people who've committed those crimes in jail. (Analyst No. 24)

> Well, as any analyst will tell you it's [the role of an analyst] probably following that intelligence cycle. So, receiving that information, you're analysing, disseminating that information, evaluating that, deciphering, there's a lot of information that comes in in an investigation. It's the ability to decipher what is relevant and what's not, and establishing those key lines of enquiry […]. All those tasks are key to providing the investigator that key intelligence support for that end goal of putting, getting that successful prosecution. (Analyst No. 7)

According to the research participants, one consequence of investigations being predominantly prosecution-oriented is that the investigations they are involved with tend to be relatively short (in terms of the amount of time spent on an investigation). This issue is discussed by several analysts:

> Operationally things are flavour of the month for a period of time, […] then the next shiny ball, or whatever, will come up. (Analyst No. 8)

> We will have our local CIU's [Crime Investigation Units] that will have a TIO or a Tactical Intelligence Officer embedded within their work unit. So, generally speaking, they will be involved with day-to-day business and if a crew or unit has got a priority job and it's all hands on, that TIO will

probably be fairly prevalent in building a lot of the background information and trying to paint the picture and support the investigators with as much understanding about the person of interest and where they sit. And often it's going to be more of a rapid response, not likely to be such a long-term investigation. [...] So, at that level an intel officer or an intel person will probably be fairly important in their collection and gathering phase, as well as providing advice to investigators, and probably not so much of a long-term perspective. (Analyst No. 17)

The prosecution-oriented and subsequently short-term nature of many law enforcement investigations has previously been noted (Bright 2017; Chiu et al. 2011; Phillips 2012). For example, Phillips (2012, p. 16) suggested that within law enforcement agencies 'the culture traditionally has valued random patrol, rapid response to service calls, and arrests of offenders over long-term focus and time-consuming inquiry needed for crime analysis'. With regard to SNA, a key impact of short-term investigations, according to many interviewees, is the restriction this places on their ability to conduct in-depth analysis. As several analysts discussed, the collection and analysis of information is not a quick process:

Analysis takes time. If you want something quickly, you'll get something that is quick and dirty, because collection takes time, evaluation takes time, analysis takes time. Actually sitting down and thinking about something and applying methodologies takes time. [...] You're dealing with people that don't want to get caught, so it's not as easy as picking up the breadcrumbs, often you can't find stuff out. (Analyst No. 7)

It can take a while to build up that knowledge to break into these networks and knowing what methods of communication they're using. [...] Sometimes that can be a slow burn, particularly with organised crime groups who are quite adept at adapting and obscuring their activities. It can be a slow burn trying to work out what they're doing and how they are approaching it [offending]. (Analyst No. 21)

Investigations that run for a relatively short amount of time impact the use of SNA in two key ways. The first, which has been documented elsewhere (Morselli and Roy 2008), is that the length and size of an investigation is likely to impact significantly on the amount of data available to analysts. Therefore, investigations may not run long enough for analysts to be able to gather sufficient relational data to conduct SNA. The second impact (an issue raised by several research participants) is that short-term investigations inhibit an analyst's ability to monitor criminal networks over time. As one analyst explained, each investigation is primarily focused on the development of a brief of evidence as quickly as possible before moving on to the next investigation. According to this analyst, one impact of moving quickly from 'job to job' is that other 'information gaps', such as the evolution of criminal networks, are regarded as secondary:

It's [monitoring the evolution of criminal networks] quite a difficult thing. […] So, in terms of how we monitor it, we monitor information that comes through our investigations […]. We have to constantly try and get information out of investigations that investigators have been investigating for a particular crime and they will go through that process of putting a brief of evidence together. But they don't necessarily then think to extract some of that information for a few other information gaps like the evolution of groups. Because of the nature of law enforcement, you move from job to job, you don't necessarily record all that information. So, it's a matter of if you want to know about the evolution of groups you've just got to keep on it, watch individuals and it's weighing up time versus jobs versus doing that sort of thing. (Analyst No. 21)

According to this analyst, because of the short-term nature of many investigation analysts have limited opportunities to monitor the evolution of criminal networks. The issue for law enforcement agencies is that it has been shown that criminal groups that adopt a loosely connected network structure are relatively resilient to disruption efforts (see Chap. 2), which according to Duijn and Klerks (2014) means that effective disruption requires a long-term focus. If law enforcement agencies wish to utilise the reported capabilities of SNA, in particular its ability to assist with the development of disruption strategies (Bright et al. 2012; Joffres and Bouchard 2015; Tayebi and Glasser 2016), analysts must be afforded the opportunity to monitor the evolution of criminal networks over a sustained period.

It should be noted that several analysts highlighted that while the majority of the investigations undertaken by their respective agencies tend to be relatively short, they certainly do run more long-term investigations. As two respondents discuss:

> When you move into some of the other areas such as the Crime Squad or taskforces […], there is often more time for them to work on those more protracted investigations. It will depend on where some of those members are. But generally, a lot of those investigations the intel will often be a driving force in relation to affecting the decision-making. Provided they are functioning well and they're able to keep the investigators and team leaders well advised of who and what fits within the scope of target for the unit and the investigation, and make some decisions about how to target them. So, they'll [intelligence analysts] often become fairly involved, particularly in those long-term investigations. We've had a couple of taskforces that have run for years and the intel has been very, very crucial. (Analyst No. 17)

> So, my role as an analyst here is looking at broader crime trends, working with the various squads on long-term projects that they don't have the time to do. (Analyst No. 22)

As these analysts suggest, long-term investigations tend to be run by specialist units or taskforces. For example, Victoria Police has the Echo Taskforce (established in 2011) which 'conducts proactive and reactive investigations involving Outlaw Motorcycle Gangs (OMCGs), and targeted investigations into identified organised crime groups' (Victoria Police 2016, p. 39). But these analysts also suggest that having a long-term focus is a luxury that many investigations do not have. Again, this limits the opportunities analysts will have to apply SNA. A further outcome of this, suggested by one analyst, is that if they do want to monitor criminal groups over time they have to do so in their own time: 'so you may not have the opportunity to be able to monitor that group once the job is closed […]. So, as an intelligence analyst it has to be self-driven in your own time' (Analyst No. 23). Overall, the short-term nature of most investigations as a result of being prosecution-oriented significantly limits the opportunities for analysts to apply SNA.

Reactive Versus Proactive Investigations

Another aspect of an investigation's focus that can impact on analysts' ability to apply SNA is whether the investigation is predominantly reactive or proactive in nature. While investigations are rarely just reactive or just proactive, as one senior analyst explained, they tend to be predominantly one or the other. This analyst also explained that intelligence analysts are required to support a wide variety of investigations that tend to fall into one of three informal categories—local crime, major crime and non-reported crime:

> I should probably start to break down the different, various types of investigations we may support, and this is by no means a formal division. But if we talk about local crime investigations, very often there are limited objectives for the investigation. There is usually a response to one reported offence or a series of offences, all committed by the same individual or group and there is usually a clear objective about what is required. There are major crime investigations in the stream that we refer to as serious crime, which includes armed robbery, homicide and several others that also are generally responsive to a particular incident, [they're] reactive investigations. Within the organised crime field, we are investigating generally crimes that are not reported to the Police. [For example,] possession, distribution, importation of various drugs typically, sometimes other contraband, the laundering of proceeds of those crimes are not reported to Police generally. They're not known to be occurring until an investigation commences and there are far more choices to be made about the sequencing and the choice of investigation targets to achieve the greatest benefit in the prevention of crime. (Analyst No. 18)

The first two investigative categories, local crime and major crime, are largely reactive: when a crime has been committed and reported, the police subsequently start an investigation. This reactive approach or 'standard model of policing' (Weisburd and Eck 2004, p. 44) has been the dominant mode within law enforcement agencies since the inception of modern day policing in 1829 (Ratcliffe 2016). The third category, non-reported crime, is far more proactive, whereby police investigate a particular group or crime problem more broadly. This category fits within intelligence-led policing (ILP) where there is a strong push to move away from the reactive model to more proactive policing (Ratcliffe 2016). Several interviewees felt SNA was best utilised in proactive investigations. This is best summarised by one analyst:

> It's [SNA] really good. I think a lot of this sort of work would be far better where it's proactive investigations, where you've got the time to really dig and you just pick your targets and then you work up your targets and you look and you're breaking down and you're trying to understand those associations. (Analyst No. 6)

This analyst identified that proactive investigations afford them more time to undertake in-depth analysis and, in particular, allow them far greater discretion when it comes to selecting their targets. It is understandable that some analysts see greater value in using SNA during proactive investigations, given that one of the main capabilities of SNA is that it can assist with the identification of suitable targets for disruption. However, only applying SNA during proactive investigations will significantly limit the opportunities analysts have to apply SNA, as law enforcement investigations remain overwhelmingly reactive (Carter 2009; Darroch and Mazerolle 2013; Gill et al. 2014; Taylor et al. 2007); this seems unlikely to change anytime soon (Ratcliffe 2016). As SNA has been shown capable of assisting in reactive investigations (see Johnson and Reitzal 2011), it is argued that analysts that restrict the use of SNA to proactive investigations are missing an opportunity to develop further insight into the offences they are investigating during predominantly reactive investigations. As this finding was only raised by a few analysts, its generalisability is limited.

Conclusion

The chapter sought to highlight how the objectives and priorities of an investigation may impact on how SNA is used and the opportunities analysts have to apply it. It was evident from the interviews that the size of an investigation, that is the number of actors being targeted, could restrict analyst's ability to apply SNA. This is because it was felt SNA was best used on large networks, but that their investigations predominantly focused on small groups. Some analysts suggested that this issue was compounded by the fact that in their view the size of the groups they are investigating are only getting smaller. The chapter also examined the rotation of analysts into different areas of investigative focus where it was found that not all areas have a need for SNA, again reducing the opportunities analysts have to apply SNA. A further issue raised by interviewees was that the investigations they are involved with are prosecution-orientated and in turn tend to be quite short. This would restrict the opportunities analysts have to conduct in-depth analysis, such as SNA which can be a time-consuming process. Finally, the chapter examined the reactive nature of the investigation analysts are often involved with. It was found that analysts were of the view that SNA is best utilised in proactive investigations where it can be used to identify further avenues of inquiry. However, it was determined that analysts that only use SNA during proactive investigations may not be using SNA to its full potential where it has been proven capable of providing insight during predominantly reactive investigations. The following chapter examines the next 'organisational characteristic of law enforcement agencies', *Working Relationships*.

References

J. Arquilla, To build a network. Prism **4**(1), 22–33 (2014)

A. Bourke, S. Doherty, O. McBride, K. Morgan, H. McGee, Female perpetrators of child sexual abuse: characteristics of the offender and victim. Psychol. Crime Law **20**(8), 769–780 (2014)

D.A. Bright, Using social network analysis to design crime prevention strategies: a case study of methamphetamine manufacture and trafficking, in *Crime prevention in the 21st century: insightful approaches for crime prevention initiatives*, ed. by B. LeClerc, E. U. Savona, (Springer International Publishing, Switzerland, 2017), pp. 143–164

D.A. Bright, C.E. Hughes, J. Chalmers, Illuminating dark networks: a social network analysis of an Australian drug trafficking syndicate. Crime Law Soc. Chang. **57**(2), 151–176 (2012)

D.L. Carter, *Law enforcement intelligence: a guide for state, local, and tribal law enforcement agencies* (2009), No. 24 July 2012. https://it.ojp.gov/documents/d/e050919201-IntelGuide_web.pdf. Accessed 21 August 2018

H. Chen, D. Zeng, H. Atabakhsh, W. Wyzga, J. Schroeder, COPLINK: managing law enforcement data and knowledge. Commun. ACM **46**(1), 28–34 (2003)

Y.-N. Chiu, B. Leclerc, M. Townsley, Crime script analysis of drug manufacturing in clandestine laboratories: implications for prevention. Br. J. Criminol. **51**(2), 355–374 (2011)

S. Darroch, L. Mazerolle, Intelligence-led policing: a comparative analysis of organizational factors influencing innovation uptake. Police Q. **16**(1), 3–37 (2013)

P.A.C. Duijn, P.P.H.M. Klerks, Social network analysis applied to criminal networks: recent developments in Dutch law enforcement, in *Networks and network analysis for defence and security*, ed. by A. J. Masys, (Springer, Heidelberg, 2014), pp. 121–159

C. Gill, D. Weisburd, C.W. Telep, Z. Vitter, T. Bennett, Community-oriented policing to reduce crime, disorder and fear and increase satisfaction and legitimacy among citizens: a systematic review. J. Exp. Criminol. **10**(4), 399–428 (2014)

L. Giommoni, A. Aziani, G. Berlusconi, How do illicit drugs move across countries? a network analysis of the heroin supply to Europe. J. Drug Issues **47**(2), 217–240 (2016)

M. Ioannou, L. Hammond, L. Machin, Male-on-male sexual assault: victim, offender and offence characteristics. J. Investig. Psychol. Offender Profiling **14**(2), 189–209 (2017)

K. Joffres, M. Bouchard, Vulnerabilities in online child exploitation networks, in *Disrupting criminal networks: network analysis in crime prevention*, ed. by G. Bichler, A. Malm, (Lynne Rienner Publishers, Boulder, CO, 2015), pp. 153–175

J.A. Johnson, J.D. Reitzal, *Social network analysis in an operational environment: defining the utility of a network approach for crime analysis using the Richmond City Police Department as a case study* (2011). http://www.coginta.org/en/document/policy_working_paper_series?page=3. Accessed 8 August 2012

M. Kenney, The architecture of drug trafficking: network forms of organisation in the Colombian cocaine trade. Global Crime **8**(3), 233–259 (2007)

C. Morselli, Hells Angels in springtime. Trends Org. Crime **12**(2), 145–158 (2009)

C. Morselli, J. Roy, Brokerage qualifications in ringing operations. Criminology **46**(1), 71–98 (2008)

S. Mullins, Social network analysis and counter-terrorism: measures of centrality as an investigative tool. Behav. Sci. Terrorism Polit. Aggression **5**(2), 115–136 (2012)

M. Natarajan, Understanding the structure of a large heroin distribution network: a quantitative analysis of qualitative data. J. Quant. Criminol. **22**(2), 171–192 (2006)

A. Perliger, A. Pedahzur, Social network analysis in the study of terrorism and political violence. Polit. Sci. Polit. **44**(2), 45–50 (2011)

S.W. Phillips, The attitudes of police managers toward intelligence-led policing. FBI Law Enforcement Bull. **81**(9), 13–17 (2012)

J. Ratcliffe, The effectiveness of police intelligence management: a New Zealand case study. Police Pract. Res. **6**(5), 435–451 (2005)

J. Ratcliffe, *Intelligence-led policing* (Routledge, New York, 2016)

C.B. Sanders, C. Weston, N. Schott, Police innovations, 'secret squirrels' and accountability: empirically studying intelligence-led policing in Canada. Br. J. Criminol. **55**(4), 711–729 (2015)

J. Scott, P. J. Carrington (eds.), *The SAGE handbook of social network analysis* (SAGE Publications, London, 2011)

J. Sheptycki, Organizational pathologies in police intelligence systems: some contributions to the lexicon of intelligence-led policing. Eur. J. Criminol. **1**(3), 307–332 (2004)

M.A. Tayebi, U. Glasser, *Social network analysis in predictive policing: concepts, models and methods* (Springer International Publishing, Switzerland, 2016)

B. Taylor, A. Kowalyk, R. Boba, The integration of crime analysis into law enforcement agencies: an exploratory study into the perceptions of crime analysts. Police Q. **10**(154), 154–169 (2007)

R.W. Taylor, A.L. Russell, The failure of police 'fusion' centers and the concept of a national intelligence sharing plan. Police Pract. Res. **13**(2), 184–200 (2012)

Victoria Police, *Annual report 2015–2016* (Victoria Police, 2016). http://www.police.vic.gov.au/content.asp?a=internetBridgingPage&Media_ID=120742. Accessed 25 April 2017

D. Weisburd, J.E. Eck, What can police do to reduce crime, disorder, and fear? Ann. Am. Acad. Polit. Soc. Sci. **593**(1), 42–65 (2004)

N.J. Wild, Prevalence of child sex rings. Pediatrics **83**(4), 553–558 (1989)

J.R. Wood, *Royal commission into the New South Wales Police Service final report volume 2: reform* (The Government of the State of New South Wales, Sydney, 1997)

6

Social Network Analysis and the Organisational Characteristics of Law Enforcement Agencies: Working Relationships

Introduction

This chapter continues on from the prior chapter by examining the second 'organisational characteristic of law enforcement agencies', *Working Relationships*. It is well known that positive working relationships are critical to the effective functioning of any organisation (Brass et al. 2004; Cohen and Prusak 2001). This is certainly true of law enforcement agencies, where it has been suggested that positive working relationships lead to improved information sharing (Carter 2009) and increased levels of trust (Schafer 2010). This was reflected by research participants who suggested that several of the working relationships within their organisations, specifically those with detectives and managers, are critical to achieving their objectives as analysts. The following chapter examines these working relationships and the impact they have on the analyst's ability to apply social network analysis (SNA).

© The Author(s) 2020
M. Burcher, *Social Network Analysis and Law Enforcement*, Crime Prevention and
Security Management, https://doi.org/10.1007/978-3-030-47771-4_6

Analysts and Detectives

The 3-I model (see Introduction to this book) identifies that the relationship between analysts and decision-makers is critical to organisations that seek to be intelligence-led (Ratcliffe 2016). As one analyst explained, the decision-maker in most investigations will usually be a detective: 'in the sense of guiding or directing the path of an investigation it has to be said first of all that the officer in charge of an investigation is almost always a detective' (Analyst No. 18). The majority of those interviewed considered their working relationship with detectives to be critical. As several analysts discuss:

So, our investigators, like I said earlier, it's important that you work hand in hand with them and it's important to have a very inclusive relationship. (Analyst No. 20)

Your collaboration with an investigator is key to make the role of intelligence as successful as it can be, as well as helping to make the investigator's case against the POI's [persons of interest] successful as well. (Analyst No. 24)

It was also clear from the majority of interviewees that during some investigations their working relationships with detectives would be characterised as positive. This is summarised by several analysts:

I'm very lucky to work with some of the most experienced detectives in the state, in this squad and our commander, he's fantastic, he appreciates what intel can do. (Analyst No. 19)

I know that in different squads there is different dynamics between teams. Some are more intelligence-led than others. The operational team that I previously worked with, it was very collaborative in terms of we had a lot of financial data that they didn't have but they had a lot of surveillance and human source data. So, it was combining those that allowed us to move forward and sort of show us what areas we needed to collect against and the same for them, what areas they needed to target. [...] So, it needs to be collaborative. (Analyst No. 23)

It depends on where you are working. The detectives that are here are currently all extremely keen and motivated. So, lots of assistance and sharing of information here and also a lot of them are, what's the word I'm looking for, new to being detectives. Therefore, they're often getting guidance from intel operatives in that we probably more guide them as opposed to the other way around. That's unique to different areas. In other areas that I have worked in it would be the other way around, detectives would really be guiding the intel operatives, it really just depends. (Analyst No. 14)

The majority of interviewees, however, also had experiences where the working relationship between themselves and detectives could be characterised as negative and, in some instances, as non-existent. This is discussed by several analysts:

[At] the divisional CIU's [Criminal Intelligence Unit] the relationships aren't that good. It's not that good with the detectives because they think what the hell do you know, get out. So, it's actually up to us to push our way into investigations. They will have debriefings and not even call us in, and then the boss says, what are you doing [analyst's name]? Nothing because they've not come to me, they haven't invited me in there, they can shove it up their ass, they're not getting anything. (Analyst No. 12)

Sounds silly but some squads you either get totally ignored by the detectives or your running around like the coffee lady, the tea lady. (Analyst No. 19)

In my observation, it depends a lot on how many prior investigations the investigator has worked on where they were supported by an intelligence officer. Many will have worked at local area commands on many investigations where they had no input from an intelligence officer or the input was limited to be more or less a data acquisition officer, if I can use that. That's not a term that describes any particular role, it's just my description of how some people might view the intelligence role. (Analyst No. 18)

There were differing views as to what contributed to such negative working relationships. For example, one analyst suggested that this may be a legacy of traditional policing practices, where intelligence analysts had little to no part in the investigation process: 'people who have come up through more traditional policing backgrounds may not necessarily have as closer relationship with the intelligence team' (Analyst No. 23). Related to this, another analyst suggested that it may in part be the result of a former practice of placing soon-to-retire officers ('dinosaurs') into intelligence positions: 'I know they're trying to get rid of the dinosaur out there. Well that's what they say, get rid of the guy that's just come to the DIU [Divisional Intelligence Unit] to retire and doesn't want to do anything' (Analyst No. 6). It has been well documented that historically intelligence analysis was often marginalised by front-line officers, detectives and senior management (Cope 2004; O'Shea and Nicholls 2002; Sanders et al. 2015; Taylor et al. 2007). Placing soon-to-retire officers into intelligence positions would contribute negatively to the value of intelligence analysis as it is perceived by detectives. Many interviewees, however, felt that one of the key factors contributing to poor working relationships between some analysts and detectives is that many investigators do not fully understand what intelligence is and, in particular, what analysts can actually do for them. This is explained by several analysts:

> Sometimes they [detectives] don't know what they want or they ask for things that aren't possible to get. You've got a system that does X, Y and Z. No, it does Y, it doesn't do Z, it doesn't do X [...]. (Analyst No. 19)

> I'm only generalising here because that's all I can [do], generalise, is that the detectives don't know what we can do for them and that's critical and sometimes jobs come in and I go what the hell, you haven't even come to see us, and yet we could have helped you solve this. Seriously, they don't know what they can do with phones half of them because phones are a very complex thing. They don't know about social networking, what we can get from there. (Analyst No. 12)

> There's a distinction often lost, particularly in policing, [...] is the difference between intelligence and evidence. Intelligence is gathered by a number of means, may or may not be admissible as evidence in a court of law, but is intended to inform decision-making and not boost prosecution. Evidence has very specific laws under which it's gathered so it can be admitted in court. A difficulty sometimes seen in law enforcement organisations is investigators confuse the two and are dissatisfied with its [intelligence

analysis] outputs because they can't use it in courts of law and they don't see the value in them as a direction-finding mechanism. (Analyst No. 14)

A lack of understanding among detectives as to what intelligence is and more broadly what their analysts can do for them is in line with previous research (Cope 2004; Phillips 2012; Ratcliffe 2005; Sanders et al. 2015). While each of these previous studies, including this study, was undertaken in different jurisdictions (the UK, the US, New Zealand, Canada and Australia respectively), they were all within organisations that have utilised intelligence-led policing (ILP) for well over a decade. Despite this, there is a clear and consistent trend showing that there has been little progress concerning the extent to which the primary clients of intelligence reports—front-line officers, detectives and senior management—understand what intelligence is and how it can support their roles. A few analysts suggested that this is perhaps less of an issue with more experienced detectives, particularly those involved in large-scale and long-term investigations. As one analyst explained in detail:

Some very inexperienced detectives who I've worked with think you can pull a rabbit out of a hat and you say sorry mate, no rabbits in this hat. There's a hat there, that's it. What do you want me to pick up in that? [...] Investigators who have been working in major crime and large-scale investigations for a long period of time have been exposed to more intel officers, often incorporate them in the internal planning of the investigation [...]. There's probably a group of investigators who have been working in major crime for a long period of time who basically like to hand pick the intelligence officers they work with and continue to use the same intelligence officers in investigations over a period of years. And I think I've heard some of them say that that is more important to them than having a choice in the investigators who will work with them, whose role is more limited and can be more easily directed. Whereas the creative thinking that they can get out of an intelligence officer who they are familiar with is something they can't replicate otherwise. (Analyst No. 19)

This analyst identified that they tended to have better working relationships with more experienced detectives and those who were subsequently in charge of specialist units or taskforces involved in large-scale/long-term investigations. That being said, it was clear that most of those interviewed had experience of negative working relationships with detectives. While the impact of such working relationships will clearly have widespread implications, this study is specifically concerned with how it may impact on the use of SNA by intelligence analysts. Given that most analysts had experiences working with detectives that did not understand what they could do for them, it is not surprising to find that several analysts had experience of providing detectives with intelligence reports that included SNA outputs, only for them not to be understood. This issue is discussed by several analysts:

> The other limitation I will say is often they [SNA outputs] are still too complicated for the general investigator to look at and really understand what they're looking at. We've handed charts over before and literally you get the response back, oh that's nice but I have no idea what that means. So often they end up too complicated. [...] You have to try and make sure it's in the simplest version as possible, you can't just assume that people look at these maps and charts with arrows and circles going everywhere, a lot of people just don't understand them. (Analyst No. 9)

> I think that's a key thing [when using SNA] because like anything, don't make it totally simplistic but make it understandable to everyone involved. (Analyst No. 13)

> You show that [link diagram] to a detective and they go, what am I looking at here and then you have to do a bit of further work [...], very often you need to snip it up into smaller parts of the bigger network. That's how you can display it to other people because otherwise you're just playing with the big fancy spider web you know, they'll come past and often make a joke. Look at you and your spider webs again or whatever. (Analyst No. 2)

If analysts are working with detectives that broadly do not understand intelligence, and specifically do not understand SNA and its outputs, it will significantly impact on the use of SNA within law enforcement agencies. As the analysts above suggest, they have to ensure that their outputs are not too complicated for detectives to understand. The concern is that analysts are being forced to simplify their intelligence outputs and in doing so compromise the integrity of their products. A similar observation was made by an analyst interviewed by Sanders et al. (2015, p. 720) who suggested that a lack of understanding among officers 'about crime analysis has left analysts having to provide simple counts of crimes, [or] "bean counting"'. It is therefore hard to imagine the primary decision-maker in an investigation, a detective, requesting that an analyst undertake SNA if they do not fully understand its findings. While not raised by interviewees, it is also possible that they are not adequately explaining the value of SNA as an investigative tool. Under the 'influence' component of the 3-I model, Ratcliffe (2016) emphasises the need for analysts to appreciate that decision-makers, including detectives, are not analytically trained and they have competing demands and constantly changing priorities (Evans 2009). The ability of analysts to effectively communicate the worth of their intelligence reports has received some attention (Evans 2009), but given the complexity of analytical tools like SNA, further research should focus specifically on them and their outputs.

A related issue is the fact that intelligence analysts have very little say, if any, when it comes to the data collected by front-line officers (Ratcliffe 2016). For example, it was noted in the Introduction to this book that it is only in an 'intelligence utopia' that analysts send out requests for information that are promptly returned (Ratcliffe 2016, p. 78). This is also in line with Duijn and Klerks' (2014, p. 150) study looking at the use of SNA within Dutch law enforcement, which noted that:

> Information gathering and processing aren't always recognized as one of the primary tasks of law enforcement officers in the frontlines of police work. This often results in poor quality of data, especially about the more circumstantial features of observed criminal cooperation and communication which are important for SNA.

One of the analysts interviewed for this study felt that if investigators were actually given training about what SNA is, and what is required to do an analysis, investigators might collect more of the relational data they need:

I think, again going back to the inputs, providing encouragement or education for on the ground investigators to gather particular kinds of data would increase the inputs available to increase the effectiveness of social network analysis. So, they can notice things that would otherwise seem innocuous about a person. If they were a member of a particular subculture, if they liked hanging around a particular spot, [this information is] sometimes captured, sometimes not. (Analyst No. 5)

Another analyst explained that they have taken it upon themselves to try and teach detectives about SNA and what its outputs mean:

A lot of the time I will turn it into a list, into an Excel list and put the filters onto it and I will also give that to the investigators with, I've managed, I've used the snipping tool to pull exactly what the meanings of Eigenvector and all the different, betweenness and connectivity and stuff that it does with a definition. And I said look, all you've got to do is filter through there, highest to lowest and this will give you, so I'm trying to teach detectives at the same time. This is the chart [link diagram] and yes, it's very pretty but it's really how these entities are weighted through these different algorithms [mathematical computations], and so I've been teaching them. […] It's a slowly, slowly approach. (Analyst No. 6)

While this point around training for detectives was only raised by a few analysts, it would suggest that the data pool from which analysts can draw from could be improved if detectives had a greater understanding of how SNA is conducted and what its capabilities are.

Analysts and Managers

Another working relationship that research participants identified as critical to undertaking their role as analysts is their relationship with their managers. Interviewees identified two informal categories of managers: 'intelligence managers' and 'senior management'. Intelligence managers or 'intelligence supervisors' (Analyst No. 7) refer to those who are directly in charge of an intelligence unit (the number of analysts under their command will vary from unit to unit). Senior managers or 'commanders'

(Ratcliffe 2005, p. 441) refers to those higher up in their organisation with a number of different units under their command, including intelligence units.[1] Both intelligence manager and operational senior management positions are staffed by sworn officers only. Similar to the working relationship between analysts and detectives, several analysts suggested that their working relationship with intelligence managers is not always ideal. For example, one analyst detailed the importance of good intelligence managers and the degree of animosity some analysts have held towards previous managers:

> Having a good intel manager who can say look, that's really not intel work, that's busy work, why are you using trained intel's [intelligence analysts] to do this when you could do that yourself or we could just get that information from anywhere. These guys have skills that should be used in a particular way [...]. Your managers have to be the sorts of managers that can use intel effectively. [...] There are people who are no longer with the organisation who I think intels [intelligence analysts] will be spitting on their graves for the next 20 years to come. (Analyst No. 19)

One analyst discussed how previously it was a requirement that intelligence managers had to have completed their organisation's internal analyst training programme, but that more recently this requirement was removed. This analyst also described the impact of this change:

> [Name of law enforcement organisation] has had a policy for a long time of I think this idea that anybody can be a manager [...] and of course that's limited. I know if somebody wanted to become a Detective Sergeant, or Detective Senior Sergeant they have to have been a Detective, they have to

---

[1] It is difficult to provide an accurate depiction of the organisational structure that exists within either Victoria Police or New South Wales Police Force for two reasons. First, their publicly available publications outlining their respective organisational structures focus on the upper levels of command (NSWPF 2017; Victoria Police 2017). Secondly, such depictions fail to accurately portray the organisational structure that does exist within law enforcement agencies, which according to Sheptycki (2017) are less hierarchical than what is shown and have a higher degree of 'fluidity'. Fluidity refers to the many horizontal and informal relations that exist within law enforcement agencies, as well as the fact that individuals in such organisations perform a variety of functions and frequently move between roles. For a detailed discussion on the organisational structure within law enforcement agencies and some of their commonalities, see Sheptycki (2017).

have qualified at Detective training school […]. For a while there [name of law enforcement organisation] required intelligence managers to have previously completed the intelligence practitioners course. Fantastic stuff, what that meant was that the people who […] are telling analysts what to do and how to do it, had done it, or at least had done the course. I know of at least one […] bloke [who] is an intelligence supervisor, but has never produced an intelligence product in his life. Has been a long-time consumer of intelligence, but has never developed it, and there were all sorts of reasons for him being picked. Don't get me wrong, great guy, good operator, excellent copper. Never developed a piece of intelligence before. So, he needs a couple of years just building his skills as an analyst and at the same time he's actually got to manage a unit and tell other people how to do their job. How does he tell people to do their job when he doesn't even know how? […] How can managers one and two up from them have any great faith that the supervisor is actually going to be able to get the best out of the analysts? (Analyst No. 7)

As this analyst suggests, if officers are placed in intelligence management positions without prior experience of producing intelligence products or having at least undertaken intelligence analysis training, it is difficult to understand how they can provide effective guidance and direction to analysts under their command. A lack of guidance and direction affects not just the use of SNA but the analyst's role more broadly. Without clear direction regarding the intelligence needs of their client (such as detectives), analysts run the risk of failing to influence decision-makers as is prescribed in the 3-I model. This finding that some intelligence managers have received little or no intelligence training supports previous research (Phillips 2012; Ratcliffe 2004). A study by Phillips (2012), which examined the attitudes of police managers within the US towards ILP, found that of the 246 participants, 30 per cent had received no guidance on intelligence analysis. The generalisability of this finding is somewhat limited, however, since the guidance given to intelligence managers is likely to vary considerably from agency to agency, and even within each organisation.

In the previous section interviewees felt that the detectives they were working with often do not understand what intelligence is and, in some cases, do not consider it to be a valuable resource. In contrast, several analysts felt that while many senior managers still do not understand what intelligence is, they regard it as critical. This is explained by one senior analyst:

> I think they [managers] understand its [intelligence] function, functionally where it fits in the process, they know they need the intelligence to advise them so they are better informed to make their decisions. [...] I think our managers have known it for a long time, but their ability to really understand how it works, they still think it's a little bit of black magic and voodoo, still getting their head around it. I think they understand its [intelligence] importance, but no, they don't understand it to the degree, again, largely because there probably hasn't been that exposure to it from the time they start all the way through [...]. Trying to give them a chart that says this is where we think offences are going to occur based on predictive modelling, they just do not understand the concept and think it's, it [the analytical chart] doesn't know what its talking about, I know better than them. So, I think there is a real disconnect in their own understanding of how intel works. So, that's something that I think needs to change over a period of time. (Analyst No. 17)

This finding is broadly in line with previous research suggesting that senior managers have been ill-prepared for the shift towards ILP, where intelligence should drive decision-making (Phillips 2012; Ratcliffe 2016; Sanders et al. 2015). For example, Ratcliffe (2016, p. 134) believes that 'we simply have not prepared the command levels of policing for the new role are being asked to perform'. The issue for analysts is that while senior managers regard intelligence to be a valuable resource in support of their decision-making, including reports derived from SNA, they still do not fully understand how such intelligence reports are developed. As one analyst explained, when senior managers have a poor understanding of tools like SNA they are unsure as to how and when it can be applied:

> The understanding of management of those concepts [SNA] [...], I tend to see a disconnect between what management might come in with, this is great theory, why aren't we doing this? And you do sort of sit down, [and say] I can probably tell you quickly that's a great idea, that parts going to fall down, you're not going to be able to get hold of that sort of information. If you do get that information, how are you going to integrate that with this other data source? (Analyst No. 8)

The lack of understanding by senior managers about analytical tools, such as SNA, is likely to have a negative impact on the use of such tools and the ability of analysts to influence decision-making.

Conclusion

The chapter provided a detailed examination of the working relationships between analysts and detectives, and analysts and managers, to determine what impact these relationships have on the application of SNA within law enforcement. It was found that the majority of analysts have experience of both positive and negative working relationships with detectives. Analysts put forward numerous explanations as to why they have had negative working relationships with detectives, including a belief that it is a historical left-over from when intelligence analysis was largely separate from the traditional investigative process. However, it was concluded that the single biggest factor influencing the relationship between analysts and detectives was the level of knowledge a detective had about intelligence. It was found that more experienced detectives had over time developed an understanding and appreciation for intelligence. This would suggest that providing greater training to junior detectives about intelligence may go some way towards improving their relationships with analysts and in turn their ability to utilise tools like SNA to their full potential. In contrast to the working relationships that analysts have had with some detectives, by in large analysts felt that senior managers recognised the value of intelligence but still do not fully understand how it is produced. It was concluded that this is in part the result of placing some individuals into managerial positions with oversight of intelligence analysts but without any analytical training. Overall, this is an area that requires further research, as a lack of understanding with regard to intelligence has a negative impact on the working relationship of analysts and managers, and in turn impacts upon the use of analytical tools like SNA. The following chapter examines the final 'organisational characteristic of law enforcement agencies', *IT Software, Systems and Training*.

References

D.J. Brass, J. Galaskiewicz, H.R. Greve, W. Tsai, Taking stock of networks and organizations: a multilevel perspective. Acad. Manage. J. **47**(6), 795–817 (2004)

D.L. Carter, *Law enforcement intelligence: a guide for state, local, and tribal law enforcement agencies* (2009), No. 24 July 2012. https://it.ojp.gov/documents/d/e050919201-IntelGuide_web.pdf. Accessed 21 August 2018

D. Cohen, L. Prusak, *In good company: how social capital makes organizations work* (Harvard Business School Press, Boston, 2001)

N. Cope, Intelligence led policing or policing led intelligence? Br. J. Criminol. **44**(2), 188–203 (2004)

P.A.C. Duijn, P.P.H.M. Klerks, Social network analysis applied to criminal networks: recent developments in Dutch law enforcement, in *Networks and network analysis for defence and security*, ed. by A. J. Masys, (Springer, Heidelberg, 2014), pp. 121–159

R.M. Evans, Influencing decision-makers with intelligence and analytical products, in *Strategic thinking in criminal intelligence*, ed. by J. Ratcliffe, (Federation Press, Sydney, 2009)

NSWPF, *Structure* (New South Wales Police Force, 2017). http://www.police.nsw.gov.au/about_us/structure. Accessed 2 August 2017

T.C. O'Shea, K. Nicholls, *Crime analysis in America* (Office of Community Oriented Policing Services, Washington, DC, 2002)

S.W. Phillips, The attitudes of police managers toward intelligence-led policing. FBI Law Enforcement Bull. **81**(9), 13–17 (2012)

J. Ratcliffe, Crime mapping and the training needs of law enforcement. Eur. J. Crim. Policy Res. **10**(1), 65–83 (2004)

J. Ratcliffe, The effectiveness of police intelligence management: a New Zealand case study. Police Pract. Res. **6**(5), 435–451 (2005)

J. Ratcliffe, *Intelligence-led policing* (Routledge, New York, 2016)

C.B. Sanders, C. Weston, N. Schott, Police innovations, 'secret squirrels' and accountability: empirically studying intelligence-led policing in Canada. Br. J. Criminol. **55**(4), 711–729 (2015)

J.A. Schafer, The ineffective police leader: acts of commission and omission. J. Crim. Just. **38**(4), 737–746 (2010)

J. Sheptycki, The police intelligence division-of-labour. Int. J. Res. **27**(6), 620–635 (2017)

B. Taylor, A. Kowalyk, R. Boba, The integration of crime analysis into law enforcement agencies: an exploratory study into the perceptions of crime analysts. Police Q. **10**(154), 154–169 (2007)

Victoria Police, *About Victoria Police* (Victoria Police, 2017). http://www.police.vic.gov.au/content.asp?Document_ID=309. Accessed 6 August 2017

7

Social Network Analysis and the Organisational Characteristics of Law Enforcement Agencies: IT Software, Systems and Training

Introduction

The third organisational characteristic of law enforcement agencies, IT software, systems and training, is arguably one of the most important factors determining whether and how well intelligence analysts can use social network analysis (SNA). While IT software and systems might be regarded as separate from the training analysts receive, in the context of this study it is evident that they are intrinsically linked. It is evident from literature that law enforcement around the world are encountering numerous challenges with their IT software and systems, as well as the associated training (Sanders and Condon 2017; Sanders and Henderson 2013; Sheptycki 2004; Whelan 2012). The chapter examines how these challenges impact on the ability of analysts to use SNA effectively.

© The Author(s) 2020   **159**
M. Burcher, *Social Network Analysis and Law Enforcement*, Crime Prevention and Security Management, https://doi.org/10.1007/978-3-030-47771-4_7

IT Software and Systems

Among the research participants there was a strong consensus that law enforcement agencies need to be keeping pace with technological changes occurring in society. This is best summarised by one analyst:

> Technology wise, we've got to be up to date, we've got to have the latest Windows [operating system], computer systems [...]. We've got to be able to have the technology to break these encrypted technologies that we're trying to keep track of. (Analyst No. 24)

This is also in line with previous research which has shown that general expectations concerning technology are influenced by what is available in society. For example, Scheepers et al. (2017) found that because single-search sites, such as Google, Bing and Wikipedia, are available publicly, there is a belief that similar functionality should exist within law enforcement, whereby staff can easily search across multiple databases. Many interviewees, however, raised concerns with the IT software and systems currently available to them:

> We've got horrendous IT systems in [name of law enforcement organisation]. (Analyst No. 1)
>
> Suitable software that works, that doesn't crash would be nice. (Analyst No. 25)
>
> Technology changes daily and we're still struggling to get information systems to work. They didn't work when we got them, and we're still struggling, and the pressure is put on the members. (Analyst No. 10)

The last analyst suggests that some of the systems they work on were not fit for purpose when they first received them. It is widely known that there are extensive challenges with the design and use of law enforcement IT software and systems in most countries, suggesting they are not unique to the organisations involved in this study (Sanders and Condon 2017; Sanders and Henderson 2013; Sheptycki 2004; Whelan 2012). That being said, research participants identified several important challenges associated with the IT software and systems available to them that may impact on their use of SNA.

Chapter 4 demonstrated how the size of criminal databases (one of the characteristics of criminal networks) and the processing capacity of network analysis software can be prohibitive for analysts wanting to examine 'large' networks. Related to this is a concern around which version of these programs analysts have access to. According to several analysts there are instances when they will only have partial functionality for a piece of software due to the prohibitive cost of purchasing full licences:

> Huge limitation is the program that you have to work with yourself. So, in [name of law enforcement organisation] we have a program, which is an American program, which if you pay a certain amount of money you get the bells and whistles and if you don't, you end up with just a certain program [with limited functionality]. (Analyst No. 3)

> I think looking at tools of social network analysis, particularly in a large organisation, there can be issues in terms of licensing, the professional tools usually have fairly expensive licenses [...]. These are the high function tools with all the fancy integrative bells and whistles that mean you can import data from anywhere, represent it in almost any way. (Analyst No. 5)

As these analysts suggest, financial constraints may impede law enforcement agencies from accessing the latest software, a factor which may prevent analysts from utilising the latest SNA methodology. An example of this is with the popular software package Analyst Notebook. While previous versions of this software allowed analysts to create second-generation link diagrams (see Chap. 3), it was only in more recent versions that third-generation mathematical computations (such as eigenvector centrality) were added to the program (Wiil 2013). Furthermore, it was noted in Chap. 3 that there are numerous mathematical calculations not yet available in analytical tools popular with law enforcement, including Analyst Notebook. It is understandable that there will be a delay between the development of new methodologies, their integration into existing or new software packages and the time at which they are made available to law enforcement. However, there was a concern among several interviewees that this delay is quite considerable, as one analyst explained: 'the approval for installing those kind of things [software] takes ages on a government network' (Analyst No. 5). This applies to both software/systems modified or developed specifically for their needs, as well as publicly available tools, such as Ucinet and Pajek (Everton 2012). The operating system used by Victoria Police provides an example of the extended delay between the release of new software or systems, and the time at which they are made available to law enforcement. It was only in 2014 that Victoria Police updated their computer network operating system from Windows XP (released in 2001) to Windows 7 (released in 2009) (Victoria Police 2014), a product that itself has now already been superseded by two newer operating systems (Windows 8 was released in 2012, while Windows 10 was released in 2015). While researchers and the private sector may have access to the latest tools and methodologies for SNA, it may be some time, even years, before law enforcement agencies can access them.

A further concern raised by most interviewees relates to the large number of software programs and systems they are required to be able to use. For example, one analyst discussed just some of the systems and programs they use:

> We need to know upwards of 40 programs. I'm not going to run through them all, but obviously we need to know all of the Microsoft products, the most that we use is through the email system, Outlook, but Word and Excel obviously to run our reports [...]. MapInfo,[1] we have a version of that adapted to our needs and that is a mapping program which as an analyst I use and yes Analyst Notebook [...]. All aspects of [Database 1][2] obviously and attached to that is SAS[3] and SAS is the Statistical Analysis System [...]. Then there's [Database 2][4] which is the intelligence database [...].

---

[1] MapInfo is a geographical information system software (Bowes 2017).

[2] Database 1 is used as this organisation's primary criminal record management database.

[3] SAS (formerly Statistical Analysis System) is a software that can analyse data in a variety of ways, including multivariate analysis and Bayesian (probability) analysis (SAS 2017).

[4] Database 2 is an 'intelligence database' (Analyst No. 3).

They're the main ones, there's others too but as you can see there's quite a few. (Analyst No. 3)

Although this includes the entire Microsoft Suite, including Outlook, Word and Excel, there are still a considerable number of programs each analyst is expected to know how to use. With regard to information systems, Victoria Police suggested that their 'current operational policing information environment comprises more than 100 processes and 10 critical systems' which involve 'laborious manual handling, data entry and duplication of effort, which in turn leads to incomplete, delayed and varied quality of data for decision support and less time for core policing duties' (Victoria Police 2014, p. 18). To emphasise this issue, the previously quoted interviewee compared the number of systems/programs they use with people they know in the private sector:

> I've talked to people in high end jobs on much more money than me and they might know 15 [programs], and okay, you know what, that's a lot. [But] people say well, to be an expert you might have people in an organisation that just do mapping or just do network analysis. (Analyst No. 3)

As this analyst suggests, it is unrealistic to expect them to be 'experts' in the use of analytical techniques like SNA and its associated software given the volume of software packages and systems they are expected to be competent in. It is evident that there are several challenges associated with the IT systems and software available to analysts that can significantly impact their ability to use SNA.

Training

In contrast, however, to the many analysts above who felt that they did not always have access to the software they needed, there were a few analysts who suggested that it is the training to utilise the software's full functionality that is lacking. This issue explained by one analyst:

The problem is these programs are coming out more sophisticated and they can do more and everyone is asking for more, and you may have more data to put through it et cetera, et cetera. But as I said, [...] my level of expertise will not be able to match the product and what it can offer. So, essentially, I'm given the keys to a Ferrari but number one, I'm driving around in a VW, and number two I'm still operating a manual whereas I should be switched on to almost operating a jumbo jet. It's just not possible I believe for us to be good enough to utilise the programs for what they can actually deliver. Do you know what I mean? [...] You sit there academically and go wow I have this fantastic system called Analyst Notebook 8, whatever it might be, there you go guys, get into it, and we sit there going, can we get some training? (Analyst No. 3)

According to this analyst, there is little benefit for law enforcement agencies investing in expensive software/system licences if they are not also willing to provide their analytical staff with upfront and ongoing training for these products. This reinforces the point that IT software, systems and training are all intrinsically linked. It is evident that partial access and functionality of the software/systems available to analysts, as well as inadequate training, limits the ability of analysts to utilise SNA to its full potential.

This issue directly relates to the type of training analysts receive and raises the question of whether the prevailing paradigm of non-specialisation or 'standard skill set' among analysts should continue (Ratcliffe 2016, p. 98). Non-specialisation refers to an expectation that analysts know how to access and use the software and systems available to them, at least on some basic level. This approach appears problematic as analytical techniques and their related software continue to become more sophisticated. Furthermore, as Ratcliffe (2016, p. 98) points out, beyond the 'standard skill set' that many analysts possess, the skills necessary for some of the more advanced analytical techniques that are applicable to intelligence analysis are increasingly found 'only in the private sector'. By not specialising and not receiving the commensurate training, analysts are only able to grasp the basics of tools like SNA and cannot master some of its more advanced techniques, such as the use of link and attribute weights (see Chap. 3). This also relates to the point made earlier in this chapter that it is common for law enforcement staff, including analysts, to regularly move around their organisation, often involving a change in the type of crime they are investigating. This limits their ability to become subject matter experts[5] in the 'genre of criminality' they are investigating, which according to Carter (2009, p. 112) is just as critical as the 'analytic methods and tools' that 'constitute the discipline of law enforcement intelligence'.

The ability to master SNA is even harder for sworn officers who, on top of their analytical training, are required to maintain a level of readiness for front-line jobs by undertaking regular training associated with such duties (Sheptycki 2017). This issue is best summarised by one analyst:

> [Name of law enforcement organisation] advertise intelligence analyst positions as 'general duties/analyst'.[6] On [the] one hand they expect an analyst to be an expert in their field with an increasingly specialised skill set which is not at all easy. And with the way technology is moving forward it requires more and more time to learn new things and do your job at a high level of overall quality. On the other hand, the organisation also expects an analyst in uniform to somehow be operational ready. But that means also staying in touch with all of the ever evolving and developing general duties policing requirements, including firearms training [...]. Effectively this is two jobs and something has to give. So, an air of mediocrity is created, counterproductive to specialising skill development at the highest level. A uniform member who is not highly trained and consistently exposed to the changing general policing environment has an unfair pressure placed on them not to make a mistake. Yet the training necessary to be competent in both roles in reality will always take something away from one or both of them, especially in today's fast paced world. [...] The organisation could also save many dollars and put more uniforms on the street if analysts were

---

[5] According to Carter (2009, p. 112), subject matter expertise includes 'understanding the motives, methods, targets, and/or commodities of criminal intelligence targets. Intelligence researchers and analysts must have subject matter knowledge of the types of enterprises that are being investigated and the context within which these enterprises occur.'

[6] 'General duties' refers to front-line police work, such as traffic patrols. These positions are not available to unsworn personnel.

converted to unsworn members who would not have the burden of having to attempt to be competent in two positions.[7] (Analyst No. 3)

According to this analyst, sworn officers are essentially doing two jobs, or at least expected to be ready to undertake either job when required. This analyst also suggests that the impact of having two jobs is that it significantly inhibits their ability to develop their analytical skill set to a high level. This supports the push within many law enforcement agencies to increase the number of unsworn analysts they have (Evans and Kebbell 2012; Fraser and Atkinson 2014; Osborne 2006). It also reinforces the argument of this study that if law enforcement organisations wish to use increasingly sophisticated tools like SNA, they need to move towards a model where their analytical staff, at least in part, become specialists in a limited number of analytical techniques.

Many interviewees suggested that one of their greatest areas of frustration is the inconsistency in the availability of their training. As the analysts quoted below explained:

> In the past, we have relied on other government departments who have got pretty well-developed training that they can share. It seems with the disintegration of the federal public service you're losing out. So, I don't know if we've got the funds or the political system to develop that ourselves but the sort of training and cross jurisdictional training that we were getting say even five years ago, doesn't exist anymore. (Analyst No. 19)

> They [training programs] came in and out of vogue, and weren't funded at different times. So sometimes we had the [software] licence but no funding for training, and other times there was no licence and no funding, and then at one stage there was. We eventually got to the point where we had licences and training funding, but the training funding was limited, so people had to get in quickly to get what they could. [...] I know there was a lot of angst years ago, when funding came for Analyst Notebook, came and went, the system was available then it wasn't available again. Then it was available

---

[7] This issue was discussed with the interviewee after the interview recording had stopped. Permission was sought to cite this conversation via email. Instead the interviewee supplied this quote with permission for it to be used.

with lots of training which was fantastic, then the training wasn't funded so we had to run our own internal course and try and show people how we did it. (Analyst No. 7)

It should be noted that this last analyst went on to say that it was their belief that things have improved in this regard within their organisation. Nonetheless, these concerns illustrate how inconsistencies in the availability of training can impact significantly on analysts' ability to carry out specific tasks, including network analysis. According to one analyst, the inconsistency in the availability of training has contributed substantially to the creation of an analytical workforce with varying levels of capability:

Analyst Notebook, it's a really good example of where the issue is. It's probably, we could class it as a Ferrari or a super car that we drive like a mini. We know that quite a number of the tools that we have access to have capabilities far beyond what the user skill levels are [...]. Back 10–15 years ago, when these tools were relatively new I was lucky enough to have an interest in getting stuck into them. Between Analyst Notebook and MapInfo and statistical things like SQL [Structured Query Language], searchers and things like that, we could actually draw out some meaningful information. I think that that's still limited to 5–10 percent of the intelligence analysts that are out there. Most of them will have a very basic understanding being able to do a simple report out of systems or a simple input into Analyst Notebook. But as far as putting in those added things like strengths [link and attribute weightings] and things like that, they just wouldn't have any idea of how to do it. (Analyst No. 8)

Inconsistencies in the availability of training contribute to the infrequent use of link and attribute weightings within law enforcement (see Chap. 4). According to several analysts, this issue is compounded by the inadequacy of the training they currently receive:

I think the limitations for it [SNA] are more on our side in terms of training for it. As I said, I've been here two years and I've only learnt about it [SNA] three months ago [...]. I think even in the training there wasn't much explanation as to the different types of centrality, what that means, and no advice on what opportunities there are for all those different types of centrality. (Analyst No. 22)

For me to be an expert, to be proficient in network analysis I need to have better training. (Analyst No. 3)

I've been trying to get [...] the level of competency up for 15 years and I don't see it changing in the next 5 minutes, and [name of law enforcement organisation] has identified that and have tried to make strides with various courses they run out of the academy. I think people understand the overall concept of social network analysis, it's not hard to grasp that. But to really get down to how we could better use that in our analysis, that's where we're probably lacking. (Analyst No. 8)

This is in line with what was noted in Chap. 4, where one analyst suggested that the underlying theories of SNA—which are critical to interpreting its outputs—are not taught to analysts. To further emphasise the need for better training for analysts, one interviewee suggested that their organisation has enough analytical staff, but what needs to change is the tools and training available to them:

When you're talking specifically on social network analysis, its actually, training would be the [...] first thing and then tools to be able to utilise that training and actually get something meaningful [...]. I even think that we've got enough, dare I say, it's always handy to have more human resources but I think we do have a large contingent of analysts out there that would be able to accomplish a lot more on a percentage basis if you gave them the right tools rather than just throwing more bodies at it. Throwing more human resources into things isn't necessarily the answer and I think that seems to be a default quite often. So, skilling them up and giving them the tools that they actually require and understanding some of the concepts. Sometimes we get bogged down and there is a disconnect between the theory that's out there and actually how we might use it. (Analyst No. 8)

This analyst suggests that law enforcement may be better served by upskilling their current analytical work force, rather than hiring more staff.

Conclusion

The chapter highlighted how limited software and systems, as well as poor training practices, can have a significant impact on the ability of analysts to use SNA. The majority of those interviewed believed their organisations were largely failing to keep up with the latest technological developments; a view that is in line with many other organisations. The result of this failure is that analysts may have access to software that has limited SNA functionality. In addition, it was found that analysts are expected to be competent in a large number of software programs in order to fulfil their role, which in turn limits their capacity to become highly knowledgeable in one or two analytical approaches, such as SNA, and their associated software. Closely linked to this issue was a view from some analysts that the training for their analytical tools is inconsistently available and at times inadequate. This issue is compounded for sworn officers who are required to maintain proficiency as 'general duties' officers and as an analyst. These issues reinforce the argument of this study that analytical workforces may need to shift away from the current standard skill-set paradigm to one of specialisation, whereby analysts become subject matter experts on a small number of analytical techniques.

References

P. Bowes, MapInfo Pro: desktop GIS, *Pitney Bowes* (2017). http://www.pitney-bowes.com/us/location-intelligence/geographic-information-systems/map-info-pro.html. Accessed 4 August 2017

D.L. Carter, *Law enforcement intelligence: a guide for state, local, and tribal law enforcement agencies* (2009), No. 24 July 2012. https://it.ojp.gov/documents/d/e050919201-IntelGuide_web.pdf. Accessed 21 August 2018

J.M. Evans, M.R. Kebbell, The effective analyst: a study of what makes an effective crime and intelligence analyst. Polic. Soc. **22**(3), 204–219 (2012)

S.F. Everton, *Disrupting dark networks* (Cambridge University Press, Cambridge, 2012)

A. Fraser, C. Atkinson, Making up gangs: looping, labelling and the new politics of intelligence-led policing. Youth Justice **14**(2), 154–170 (2014)

D. Osborne, *Out of bounds: innovation and change in law enforcement intelligence analysis* (Joint Military Intelligence College, Washington, DC, 2006)

J. Ratcliffe, *Intelligence-led policing* (Routledge, New York, 2016)

C. Sanders, C. Condon, Crime analysis and cognitive effects: the practice of policing through flows of data. Global Crime **18**(3), 237–255 (2017)

C.B. Sanders, S. Henderson, Police 'empires' and information technologies: uncovering material and organisational barriers to information sharing in Canadian police services. Polic. Soc. **23**(2), 243–260 (2013)

SAS, *SAS/STAT software* (SAS, 2017). https://www.sas.com/en_us/software/stat.html. Accessed 5 August 2017

R. Scheepers, C. Whelan, I. Nielsen, M. Burcher, *Integrated law enforcement project: qualitative end-user evaluation* (Deakin University, Geelong, 2017)

J. Sheptycki, Organizational pathologies in police intelligence systems: some contributions to the lexicon of intelligence-led policing. Eur. J. Criminol. **1**(3), 307–332 (2004)

J. Sheptycki, The police intelligence division-of-labour. Int. J. Res. Policy **27**(6), 620–635 (2017)

Victoria Police, *Victoria Police blue paper: a vision for Victoria Police 2025* (Victoria Police, 2014). http://www.police.vic.gov.au/content.asp?Document_ID=42063. Accessed 14 December 2016

C. Whelan, *Networks and national security: dynamics, effectiveness and organisation* (Ashgate, London, 2012)

U.K. Wiil, *Issues for the next generation of criminal network investigation tools*. Paper presented to European Intelligence and Security Informatics Conference, Uppsala, Sweden, 2013

8

Conclusion: Social Network Analysis and the Characteristics of Criminal Networks and Law Enforcement

Introduction

The environment in which law enforcement must operate has seen considerable change occur over the past two decades. This has included society entering the 'information age' (Arquilla 2014; Castells 2004) and a blurring of the lines between law enforcement and national security (Coyne and Bell 2011; Dupont 2015; Stainer 2013). There has also been the emergence of 'new' crime types, such as cybercrime (Taylor et al. 2014). Combined with evidence to suggest that criminal groups are increasingly operating in highly flexible and loosely connected networks (Bright et al. 2012; Kenney 2007; Natarajan 2006), it is understandable that both researchers and analysts have looked to utilise social network analysis (SNA), with its reported capabilities to provide insight into the structure of such groups, as well as the position of critical actors (Schwartz and Rouselle 2009; Strang 2014; van der Hulst 2009). However, given the large body of literature that has examined the use of SNA as an investigative tool (Masys 2014; Morselli 2014), it is somewhat surprising that we know almost nothing about its use by law enforcement—those who arguably stand to gain most from its application. As outlined in the

© The Author(s) 2020
M. Burcher, *Social Network Analysis and Law Enforcement*, Crime Prevention and
Security Management, https://doi.org/10.1007/978-3-030-47771-4_8

Introduction to this book, without understanding the use of SNA within operational law enforcement environments, particularly those that have looked to adopt the increasingly popular business model of intelligence-led policing (ILP) (Ratcliffe 2016), we cannot hope to advance SNA to the 'next level' as an analytical tool for crime intelligence (Mullins 2012, p. 19).

This study has provided an extensive analysis of SNA and its application in operational law enforcement environments. This analysis had two principal objectives: (1) to identify whether SNA is being used by intelligence analysts in operational law enforcement environments in Australia, and if so how; and (2) to determine what challenges intelligence analysts face when applying network analysis concepts and techniques to criminal networks. Due to the exploratory nature of this research this study utilised semi-structured interviews for their well-documented ability to provide enough structure to address key research questions while remaining flexible enough to allow interviewees to provide new insights (Galletta 2013). Drawing on interviews with 27 intelligence analysts from two Australian state law enforcement agencies, this study has contributed significantly to both the SNA and intelligence literature. While other studies have presented the views of intelligence analysis (Cope 2004; John and Maguire 2004; Ratcliffe 2005), they have tended to examine much broader topics, such as intelligence and ILP. This book is unique in that it has concentrated on just one analytical tool, SNA, from the perspective of those directly engaged in its application within operational environments. It is argued that this provides a greater depth of insight into the topic under investigation. In doing so, this study also constitutes the first study to examine the use of SNA by law enforcement in Australia. The analysis presented in this book highlights that while SNA remains a valuable addition to an analyst's toolbox, there are numerous challenges that must be overcome, many of which have received almost no attention.

This final chapter acts as a discussion and conclusion to this book and is divided into three sections. The first section reviews how this study has advanced our understanding of whether and how SNA is being used in operational law enforcement environments. The second section looks at the contribution this study has made to our understanding of the characteristics of criminal networks, the core challenges of applying SNA to criminal networks according to the existing SNA literature. The third section focuses on the primary contribution of this study, the organisational characteristics of law enforcement agencies—a collection of challenges that arguably can inhibit the ability of analysts to apply SNA just as much as the often-cited characteristics of criminal networks. It is also argued in this section that this study has made a number of contributions to the broader intelligence literature where significant insight has been provided with regard to the use of intelligence and how it is perceived within law enforcement. Finally, this conclusion outlines the limitations of this study as well as key areas requiring further research.

Whether and How Analysts Apply Social Network Analysis

Researchers have applied SNA to an extensive array of criminal networks. This includes networks involved in terrorism (Krebs 2002), the manufacture and distribution of illicit drugs (Natarajan 2006), fraud (Nash et al. 2013), the illicit art trade (Bichler et al. 2013), youth gangs (Bouchard and Konaraski 2014), violent crime (Papachristos 2009) and gun trafficking (Leuprecht and Aulthouse 2014). While much of this literature highlights the various ways in which law enforcement may benefit from the use of SNA (Berlusconi 2017; Bright et al. 2015a; Morris and Deckro 2013), outside of countries such as the Netherlands (Duijn and Klerks 2014), it is largely unknown if law enforcement agencies in other jurisdictions, such as Australia, are using SNA. This is a critical gap in understanding, given that law enforcement agencies stand to benefit greatly from the use of SNA.

To better understand whether SNA is being used by crime intelligence analysts, specifically those in Australia, this study utilised Klerks' (1999) three generations of network analysis development. While a few analysts still use first-generation network analysis—that is, drawing who is connected to whom in a criminal network on a whiteboard—all remaining interviewees have moved on to the second or third generations of network analysis. When it comes to second-generation network analysis, which involves the partial automation of the network analysis process through the use of software, there was a concern among interviewees that too much emphasis was placed on the layout of link diagrams (e.g., to ensure that the 'dots' and 'lines' are not overlapping) and at times not enough on the actual relationships. The reliance on a visual interpretation of the link diagram is a fundamental limitation of first- and second-generation network analysis, given that it has been shown people mistakenly correlate an actor's physical position in a link diagram with their actual position within that network (McGrath et al. 1997; McGrath et al. 2003). With regard to the third generation of network analysis, or SNA, the majority of interviewees considered it to be a valuable tool capable of guiding investigations and overcoming cognitive biases. The impact of cognitive biases has been well documented (Berlusconi 2013; Bichler et al. 2016; Rossmo 2009); therefore, recognition among those interviewed that SNA can help mitigate cognitive bias is a critical finding. Interviews with intelligence analysts in two Australian jurisdictions confirm that Australian intelligence professionals do use SNA as an investigative tool.

In the limited instances where it is known that law enforcement use SNA (Duijn and Klerks 2014; Johnson and Reitzal 2011), we know little about *how* it is being used. For example, the study by Johnson and Reitzal (2011) primarily focuses on several case studies in which the Richmond City Police Department use SNA. But as Sheptycki (2017, p. 3) suggested, a 'typical' law enforcement agency has many responsibilities (e.g., investigations, traffic enforcement and policing protests), as well as numerous units tasked with responding to these issues. It is therefore a significant limitation of the existing literature that there has not been a more in-depth examination of the use of SNA by law enforcement intelligence analysts across an entire agency. This study has filled this critical gap in understanding. Consistent with the findings in the broader literature, some analysts interviewed for this study reported using SNA to identify possible points of vulnerability within criminal networks. Many analysts were simply using SNA as a way of identifying further avenues of enquiry. This suggests there is a slight difference in the way in which SNA is being used by researchers—who tend to be concerned with identifying points of vulnerability (Bright et al. 2014; Malm and Bichler 2011;

Morselli 2010)—and analysts, who appear to be more concerned with the identification of information gaps and finding persons of interest previously unknown to detectives. This has implications for research going forward. In order for SNA to continue to develop as an investigative tool it is important that we gain a greater understanding of the motivations behind its use by law enforcement agencies.

This study has advanced understanding of link and attribute weights and their use by intelligence analysts. While some analysts looked to incorporate link weightings (such as frequency of contact), no analyst used any form of formal attribute weighting (such as the relative strength of the knowledge and/or resources each actor brings to a network). Again, this is reflective of the broader SNA literature where the use of link weightings (Krebs 2002; Leuprecht and Hall 2013), and in particular attribute weightings (Bright et al. 2015b; Hofmann and Gallupe 2015), remains relatively rare. For researchers this is not surprising given that the data they have predominantly used is only what is publicly available, which is often insufficient to apply these weightings (Medina 2014). Alternatively, as those interviewed suggest, analysts are often working with data that is regarded as intelligence, not evidence, and only the latter tends to become publicly available. Analysts are therefore likely to have access to far larger datasets, meaning that they arguably have greater opportunities to utilise the capabilities of SNA than researchers. It is surprising then that they appear to apply link and attribute weights just as infrequently as researchers. The question then becomes: why are analysts not using link and attribute weights more often? One explanation is that analysts do not receive adequate training to undertake such forms of analysis (discussed in greater detail later in this chapter). Another explanation, as suggested by several interviewees, is that despite access to greater volumes of data, they often still lack access to the types of relational data needed to apply such weightings. Overall, though, this is an area that requires further research as link and attribute weightings will generally provide greater insight into the network under investigation (Bright et al. 2015b).

This study is also the first to provide an in-depth examination of *when*, during an investigation, SNA should be applied. Among the research participants there was little consensus concerning this issue, with analysts suggesting that SNA is best utilised anywhere, from the start of an investigation through to presenting intelligence findings in a courtroom. Interviewees highlighted a number of considerations they must make when deciding when to apply SNA. Using SNA at the start of an investigation can provide a unit or taskforce with guidance around who to focus their attention on; however, there is the possibility of increased levels of error entering the analysis, as analysts may not have sufficient time or information to determine the relevance of the data being used at that stage. Alternatively, several of those interviewed suggested that using SNA throughout an investigation can allow analysts to determine the value of new information as it comes in, as well as help to mitigate one of the core challenges of applying SNA, the dynamic nature of social networks. The problem of using SNA throughout is that it is a very time-consuming process (Duijn and Klerks 2014). It was also suggested that there is an opportunity being lost within law enforcement agencies by not applying SNA at the conclusion of investigations to help evaluate the actions they have taken, as well as potentially guiding the development of new investigations. This is likely to be a highly beneficial approach for law enforcement, given that those interviewed emphasised that their investigations are usually not entirely discrete, with current suspects often showing up in future cases. Finally, it was noted that the outputs of SNA, particularly the link diagrams, are often presented in a courtroom. While this is regarded as a useful way of demonstrating a criminal network, many analysts highlighted the difficulty in creating a link diagram that meets the strict evidentiary requirements of a court. Furthermore, several analysts suggested that there is a risk that those involved in a court case, from the jury through to the lawyers, may not fully understand the outputs of SNA. Future research should explore the use of SNA within the courts, focusing on whether its outputs are understood and what impact they may have.

The Characteristics of Criminal Networks in Operational Environments

Sparrow's (1991) seminal paper was one of the first to encourage a collaboration between network theorists and intelligence analysis. He argued intelligence analysis would benefit greatly from the methods and techniques inherent in network analysis. Sparrow also emphasised that it would not be a simple case of applying existing network analysis methodologies to criminal networks, and that there would be numerous challenges to overcome. He referred to these challenges as the 'characteristics of criminal networks'. The first characteristic, *size*, refers to the fact that law enforcement agencies often have very large databases and that it may not be possible to process such datasets. The second characteristic, *incompleteness*, concerns the inevitability that criminal databases will have missing data. While not raised by Sparrow (1991), many subsequent studies have highlighted other 'data challenges', which include *incorrectness*, *inconsistency* and *data transformation* (Morris and Deckro 2013; Xu and Chen 2005). The third characteristic, *fuzzy boundaries*, relates to the difficulty in determining which actors and relationships are to be included in an analysis. The fourth characteristic, *dynamic*, refers to the fact that a network's structure is often in a state of change.

This study sought to expand the current understanding of the challenges analysts face when applying SNA to criminal networks by examining them from the perspective of current users. Interviewees emphasised the increase in the amount of data their agencies are required to collect and the number of sources they are expected to obtain it from, resulting in incredibly large criminal databases. This finding is consistent with previous research (Décary-Hétu and Dupont 2012; Joh 2014). Interviewees also highlighted several limitations of working with large datasets, including that these can create a great deal of distraction for the analyst, and that when incorporated into SNA the link diagram that is produced becomes rather meaningless as the image will simply involve a blur of intersecting lines. Analysts reported that one of the primary concerns with regard to criminal databases is the fact that software packages available to them are unable to process large quantities of information. While the processing capacity of computers and the software used to conduct SNA has advanced considerably, it appears that this has either been matched by, or possibly surpassed, the volume of data collected by law enforcement agencies. The impact for analysts is that there are restrictions on the size of the networks they examine.

This study has contributed to the body of knowledge regarding SNA data challenges in a number of ways. Initially, this study examined the issue of incompleteness. Research participants were well aware of the challenges associated with incomplete data. One analyst raised concerns about how they regularly use information collected from previous investigations in a current investigation. This analyst was concerned that using this type of data, which might have been collected for different purposes, may impact upon the findings of SNA. While only raised by one analyst this is an issue that requires further attention as it has implications both for analysts, who derive much of their information from their existing data holdings, and for researchers, who primarily obtain their information from publicly available law enforcement data (e.g., once it has gone through the courts). In line with some of the SNA literature (Morris and Deckro 2013; Xu and Chen 2005), this study also explored several other data challenges associated with applying SNA to criminal networks, including incorrectness, inconsistency and data transformation. Again, interviewees were well aware that their data holdings would not always be correct and/or consistent. Several research participants noted that it is common practice for intelligence analysts to apply a formal reliability and validity weighting to the information they use in an effort to mitigate issues concerning incorrectness. While many researchers advocate trying to obtain information from more than one source to help ensure the accuracy of the data used (Colladon and Remondi 2017; Duijn et al. 2014; Xu et al. 2004), formal reliability and validity weightings are not common within the SNA literature and there is little consistency around what data is used and its accuracy (Bright et al. 2012; Morris and Deckro 2013). It is argued that researchers would benefit from incorporating reliability and validity weightings into their studies, particularly those that include relational data derived from sources that have not passed through the police and the courts.

Fuzzy boundaries are regarded within the SNA literature as one of the primary challenges to applying SNA to criminal networks (Belli et al. 2015; Berlusconi 2013; Décary-Hétu and Dupont 2012; Leuprecht et al. 2015). No study to date, however, had examined how intelligence analysts approached this issue. Only one analyst mentioned any use of a formal boundary-specification rule. All remaining analysts appear to simply define the boundary of a network based on whatever information is available. While the mathematical computations inherent in SNA are relatively robust to errors in the boundary of a network (Borgatti et al. 2006; Xu and Chen 2008), boundary specification remains a primary concern for both researchers and analysts. Therefore, this study examined the different boundary-specification rules that have been used by researchers to determine which are likely to be of use to intelligence analysts. It was found that while no boundary-specification rule should be excluded entirely, a nominalist approach (where an analyst puts in place a conceptual framework to achieve their own analytical objectives) that uses either a relation or an activity definitional focus are likely to be the most appropriate for the networks they are investigating.

With regard to Sparrow's final characteristic, the dynamic nature of criminal networks, interviewees were aware of the challenges this issue creates. Several analysts emphasised that one of the key differences of applying SNA retrospectively (Burcher and Whelan 2015; Calderoni 2014; Natarajan 2006)—compared with trying to apply it in 'real-time' as an investigation unfolds—is the difficulty in keeping their knowledge up to date. For example, several analysts noted how they had seen SNA charts created, only to be informed that they were out of date. This is an important finding, as it emphasises how challenging it can be for analysts to apply SNA in operational environments. Directly related to this issue is the rate at which criminal networks change, with several analysts suggesting that criminal networks are becoming even more dynamic. In their eyes, this is occurring due to a willingness among criminals to prioritise monetary gain over other concerns (such as ethnic rivalries) and the ease with which they can now communicate through certain technology (such as instant messaging apps). This would suggest that when applying SNA longitudinally, it would be advisable for both researchers and analysts to have relatively short time periods between each analysis (e.g., monthly), as opposed to years, which has been the norm (Bright and Delaney 2013; Helfstein and Wright 2011). Furthermore, it is recommended that law enforcement agencies wanting to monitor the changes that occur within criminal networks should develop an 'active library' whereby relational data from multiple sources is regularly combined into a usable format for SNA.

The Impact of the Organisational Characteristics of Law Enforcement Agencies

The majority of the existing literature consists of case studies whereby SNA is applied to a particular criminal network, often years after they were in operation (Everton and Cunningham 2015; Harris-Hogan 2012). This is understandable, given the well-documented difficulties researchers face in gaining access to law enforcement data, primarily due to security concerns (Klerks 1999; Krebs 2002). This has even encouraged some researchers to look at innovative ways of obtaining relational data, as is the case with Bright et al. (2012) who were able to derive sufficient relational data from judges' sentencing comments in order to map an illicit drugs network. However, applying SNA to a criminal network that operated some time ago, compared with undertaking 'real-time' analysis in an operational environment where new information is regularly collected, are two very different propositions. Furthermore, it is well known that law enforcement agencies have a number of organisational characteristics, including having policies of withholding intelligence based on the 'need-to-know' principle (Carter 2009; NCPE 2005), being predominantly reactive (Taylor et al. 2007) and being prosecution-oriented (Ratcliffe 2016). This is the first study to provide a fulsome examination of the potential impact of the organisational environment in which intelligence analysts operate on their ability to use SNA.

This study has advanced understanding of how SNA can be adopted as a crime intelligence tool by highlighting three organisational characteristics of law enforcement agencies and the challenges they present for intelligence analysts. The first of these is *Investigative Focus*. As with much of the broader SNA literature (Burcher and Whelan 2015; Mullins 2012; Perliger and Pedahzur 2011; Scott and Carrington 2011), many of those interviewed felt that SNA is best utilised on 'large' networks. While there is no consistency in the literature with regard to what this is (Mainas 2012; Stollenwerk et al. 2016), several interviewees suggested that it referred to networks consisting of approximately 50 actors. Research participants also suggested that they have limited opportunities to apply SNA as the cases they are investigating regularly involve few actors (e.g., less than 50 actors). It was suggested that this is heavily influenced by the type of crime being investigated—for example, sex offences are often committed by lone actors. The impact of this for analysts is that they can go many months without using SNA, and subsequently when they do they struggle due to a lack of practice. Despite this, it is suggested that analysts who restrict the use of SNA to large networks are missing an opportunity to develop further insight into smaller criminal groups, where research has shown SNA can provide much insight (Burcher and Whelan 2015; Koschade 2006; Krebs 2002; Leuprecht et al. 2015; Varese 2013).

Interviewees emphasised that the focus of the investigations they are involved with is predominantly on obtaining a prosecution, and that their role is to assist in achieving this objective. The impact of this, as suggested by many analysts, is that the investigations they are involved with tend to be relatively short, limiting their ability to conduct in-depth analysis. Critically, interviewees felt that this restricted their ability to monitor criminal networks over time through longitudinal SNA. It has been shown that because criminal networks are highly adaptive, a long-term approach to their disruption is required (Duijn and Klerks 2014). By having limited opportunities to monitor criminal networks over time, analysts are unable to utilise SNA to its full potential. The research participants noted that the majority of the investigations they are involved with are reactive in nature. They also felt, however, that SNA is best utilised in proactive investigations. Analysts that limit their use of SNA to proactive investigations may be missing an opportunity to develop insight into criminal networks when conducting predominantly reactive investigations. This also supports the wider finding of this study that the investigative focus of many law enforcement investigations means that intelligence analysts have limited opportunities to apply SNA.

The second organisational characteristic of law enforcement agencies examined by this study was *Working Relationships*. This study identified several ways in which working relationships can impact on the ability of analysts to achieve their objectives. Many analysts highlighted that those in charge of an investigation will almost always be detectives, and that their working relationship is critical to achieving their objectives as analysts. While all interviewees highlighted positive working experiences with some detectives, almost all also suggested that at times these relationships can be less than ideal, and in some cases non-existent. Research participants put forward several reasons for this, but the most common was a lack of understanding among detectives about what intelligence is and how it is produced. This finding supports previous research (Cope 2004; Phillips 2012; Ratcliffe 2005; Sanders et al. 2015) and shows a clear and consistent trend whereby there has been little progress concerning the extent to which front-line officers, detectives and managers understand what intelligence is and what it can do for them. Interviewees felt that the impact of this lack of understanding among detectives meant there were times when they have produced intelligence reports, including SNA outputs, that were simply not understood by the detective in charge of the investigation. This would suggest that unless detectives improve their understanding of intelligence, it will be difficult for analysts to disseminate their more complicated reports, including SNA.

Interviewees also highlighted the importance of positive working relationships with intelligence managers and senior management. Although only noted by one analyst, it was highlighted that within their organisation there is no requirement that intelligence managers complete any form of intelligence training. This analyst felt that it would not be possible for a manager without such training to best utilise the people under their command. It was suggested that while senior managers within their organisations understand the importance of intelligence, they still do not understand how it is produced. Therefore, while senior managers recognise the worth of SNA, they do not understand how and when it can be used. A focus of this study was on the impact that negative relationships can have on the use of SNA. It is important to also note, however, that the lack of knowledge among managers with regard to intelligence has implications not just for SNA but for the extent to which law enforcement agencies become truly intelligence-led. While this study has advanced our knowledge of the working relationships within law enforcement, future research should look to gather the perceptions of detectives and managers to develop further insight in this area.

The third organisational characteristic of law enforcement agencies examined by this study was *IT Software and Systems*. This study confirms previous research (Sanders and Henderson 2013; Sheptycki 2004; Whelan 2012), with those interviewed highlighting that the limitations of the IT software, systems and training available to them pose numerous challenges. One concern raised by many analysts is that they regularly have delayed access to certain systems and software (both licenced and open-source), with this often the result of budgetary constraints. While the need for secure systems would explain why there would be some delay in law enforcement agencies accessing these systems and software, interviewees suggested that this delay is often many years. As SNA is not to be regarded as a finished methodology but as one that continues to develop (see Schwartz and Rouselle 2009), law enforcement agencies may not have access to the latest tools and methodologies for a considerable amount of time.

Another concern raised by many interviewees is the number of software packages and systems in which they are expected to demonstrate competence. What complicates this issue, according to the research participants, is that these products are increasingly sophisticated, meaning that many cannot utilise the full functionality of these tools. It was suggested by one analyst that it is even more difficult for sworn officers to master tools like SNA when they essentially have to maintain training for two jobs. Law enforcement agencies may be better served by adopting a model whereby their analytical staff, at least in part, specialise in a limited number of analytical tools. Arguably, what appears to frustrate interviewees most is the inconsistency and quality of the training they receive. Several analysts suggested that one of the impacts of this is analytical staff with wide-ranging levels of capability. To emphasise how much of an issue this is, one analyst suggested that their organisation would be better served by upskilling their current analysts, rather than hiring more staff.

Final Comments

This study has advanced understanding of SNA as an investigative tool for crime intelligence. There are, however, several critical areas that require further research. The use of semi-structured interviews with intelligence analysts has proven to be a highly effective way of gaining insight from what can be at times a hard-to-reach population, law enforcement agencies. The limitation of this study is that the generalisability of the findings is limited due to the number of law enforcement agencies involved in the study. The research methodology used in this study should be applied to other jurisdictions, and other levels of law enforcement (such as local, state and federal policing, depending on the jurisdiction), in order to develop further insight into the use of SNA within operational environments. For example, while it would be expected that the organisational characteristics of law enforcement agencies would be found in other jurisdictions, their relative impact on the ability of analysts to apply SNA would likely vary considerably. Furthermore, it is possible that other organisational characteristics exist in other jurisdictions. When undertaking this type of research, future studies should look to follow the approach used by this study, whereby analysts were included from a wide variety of units/taskforces (such as specialist squads that focus on a particular category of crime) to help develop further knowledge as to which areas/offences SNA might be most applicable. This is critical given the wide variety of responsibilities law enforcement agencies have, and the numerous units/taskforces that even law enforcement agencies of moderate size use to respond to these issues. Further investigation of the use of SNA within operational law enforcement environments will continue the development of SNA as an investigative tool.

As a result of this study, it is evident that there is a pressing need for further insight into the perspectives of detectives and managers regarding SNA, and the role of intelligence more broadly. Detectives and managers are primary decision-makers, meaning they have a great deal of influence over the type of work undertaken by analysts and the actions taken as a result of their intelligence reports. Specifically, they are likely to be the primary recipients of any SNA outputs. It is therefore critical that we develop a more detailed understanding of the intelligence needs within law enforcement settings, and the specific means by which SNA can enhance analytical processes. This would provide a more complete picture of the use of SNA in operational environments.

It was clear that interviewees saw value in SNA as an investigative tool, including its ability to identify key actors and further avenues of enquiry. Its use within operational environments as it currently stands is perhaps best summarised by one analyst: 'between the availability of data, the people, the competency level of the people looking at it and the tools they've got to use […], it makes the theory very hard to accomplish in the real world'.

References

J. Arquilla, To build a network. *PRism* **4**(1), 22–33 (2014)

R. Belli, J.D. Freilich, S.M. Chermak, K.A. Boyd, Exploring the crime–terror nexus in the United States: a social network analysis of a Hezbollah network involved in trade diversion. *Dyn. Asymmetric Confl.* **8**(3), 263–281 (2015)

G. Berlusconi, Do all the pieces matter? assessing the reliability of law enforcement data sources for the network analysis of wire taps. *Glob. Crime* **14**(1), 61–81 (2013)

G. Berlusconi, Social network analysis and crime prevention, in *Crime prevention in the twenty-first century: insightful approaches for crime prevention initiatives*, ed. by B. Leclerc, E. U. Savona, (Springer International Publishing, Switzerland, 2017), pp. 129–141

G. Bichler, S. Bush, A. Malm, Bad actors and faulty props: unlocking legal and illicit art trade. *Glob. Crime* **14**(4), 359–385 (2013)

G. Bichler, S. Lim, E. Larin, Tactical social network analysis: using affiliation networks to aid serial homicide investigation. *Homicide Stud.* **21**(2), 133–158 (2016)

S.P. Borgatti, K.M. Carley, D. Krackhardt, On the robustness of centrality measures under conditions of imperfect data. *Soc. Networks* **28**(2), 124–136 (2006)

M. Bouchard, R. Konaraski, Assessing the core membership of a youth gang from its co-offending network, in *Crime and networks*, ed. by C. Morselli, (Routledge, New York, 2014), pp. 81–93

D.A. Bright, J.J. Delaney, Evolution of a drug trafficking network: mapping changes in network structure and function across time. *Glob. Crime* 14(2–3), 238–260 (2013)

D.A. Bright, C. Greenhill, N. Levenkova, Dismantling criminal networks: can node attributes play a role? in *Crime and networks*, ed. by C. Morselli, (Routledge, New York, 2014), pp. 148–162

D.A. Bright, C. Greenhill, M. Reynolds, A. Ritter, C. Morselli, The use of actor-level attributes and centrality measures to identify key actors: a case study of an Australian drug trafficking network. *J. Contemp. Crim. Justice* 31(3), 262–278 (2015a)

D.A. Bright, C. Greenhill, A. Ritter, C. Morselli, Networks within networks: using multiple link types to examine network structure and identify key actors in a drug trafficking operation. *Glob. Crime* 16(3), 1–19 (2015b)

D.A. Bright, C.E. Hughes, J. Chalmers, Illuminating dark networks: a social network analysis of an Australian drug trafficking syndicate. *Crime Law Soc. Chang.* 57(2), 151–176 (2012)

M. Burcher, C. Whelan, Social network analysis and small group 'dark' networks: an analysis of the London bombers and the problem of 'fuzzy' boundaries. *Glob. Crime* 16(2), 104–122 (2015)

F. Calderoni, Identifying mafia bosses from meeting attendance, in *Networks and network analysis for defence and security*, ed. by A. J. Masys, (Springer International Publishing, Cham, Germany, 2014), pp. 27–48

D.L. Carter, *Law enforcement intelligence: A guide for state, local, and tribal law enforcement agencies* (2009). https://it.ojp.gov/documents/d/e050919201-IntelGuide_web.pdf. Accessed 21 August 2018.

M. Castells, *The network society* (Edward Elgar Publishing, Cheltenham, UK, 2004)

A.F. Colladon, E. Remondi, Using social network analysis to prevent money laundering. *Expert Syst. Appl.* 67, 49–58 (2017)

N. Cope, Intelligence led policing or policing led intelligence? *Br. J. Criminol.* 44(2), 188–203 (2004)

J.W. Coyne, P. Bell, Strategic intelligence in law enforcement: A review. *J. Polic. Intell. Count. Terror.* 6(1), 23–39 (2011)

D. Décary-Hétu, B. Dupont, The social network of hackers. *Glob. Crime* 13(3), 160–175 (2012)

P.A.C. Duijn, V. Kashirin, P.M.A. Sloot, The relative ineffectiveness of criminal network disruption. *Sci. Rep.* 4(4238), 1–15 (2014)

P.A.C. Duijn, P.P.H.M. Klerks, Social network analysis applied to criminal networks: recent developments in Dutch law enforcement, in *Networks and network analysis for defence and security*, ed. by A. J. Masys, (Springer, Heidelberg, 2014), pp. 121–159

B. Dupont, Security networks and counter-terrorism: a reflection on the limits of adversarial isomorphism, in *Social networks, terrorism and counter-terrorism: radical and connected*, ed. by M. Bouchard, (Routledge, London, 2015), pp. 155–174

S.F. Everton, D. Cunningham, Dark network resilience in a hostile environment: optimizing centralization and density. *Criminol. Crim. Justice Law Soc.* **16**(1), 1–20 (2015)

A. Galletta, *Mastering the semi-structured interview and beyond: from research design to analysis and publication* (New York University Press, New York, 2013)

S. Harris-Hogan, The Australian Neojihadist network: origins, evolution and structure. *Dyn. Asymmetric Confl.* **5**(1), 18–30 (2012)

S. Helfstein, D. Wright, Covert or convenient? evolution of terror attack networks. *J. Confl. Resolut.* **55**(5), 785–813 (2011)

D.C. Hofmann, O. Gallupe, Leadership protection in drug-trafficking networks. *Glob. Crime* **16**(2), 123–138 (2015)

E.E. Joh, Policing by numbers: big data and the fourth amendment. *Wash. Law Rev.* **89**(1), 35–68 (2014)

T. John, M. Maguire, *The national intelligence model: key lessons from early research*, Home Office (2004). http://library.npia.police.uk/docs/hordsolr/rdsolr3004.pdf. Accessed 6 March 2012.

J.A. Johnson, J.D. Reitzal, *Social network analysis in an operational environment: defining the utility of a network approach for crime analysis using the Richmond City Police Department as a case study* (2011). http://www.coginta.org/en/document/policy_working_paper_series?page=3. Accessed 8 August 2012.

M. Kenney, The architecture of drug trafficking: network forms of organisation in the Colombian cocaine trade. *Glob. Crime* **8**(3), 233–259 (2007)

P. Klerks, The network paradigm applied to criminal organisations: theoretical nitpicking or relevant doctrine for investigators? Recent developments in the Netherlands. *Connections* **24**(3), 53–65 (1999)

S. Koschade, A social network analysis of Jemaah Islamiyah: the applications to counterterrorism and intelligence. *Stud. Confl. Terror.* **29**(6), 559–575 (2006)

V. Krebs, Mapping networks of terrorist cells. *Connect* **24**(3), 43–52 (2002)

C. Leuprecht, A. Aulthouse, Guns for hire: North America's intra-continental gun trafficking networks. *Criminol. Crim. Justice Law Soc.* **15**(3), 57–74 (2014)

C. Leuprecht, K. Hall, Networks as strategic repertoires: functional differentiation among Al-Shabaab terror cells. *Glob. Crime* **14**(2–3), 287–310 (2013)

C. Leuprecht, O. Walther, D.B. Skillicorn, H. Ryde-Collins, *Hezbollah's global tentacles: a relational approach to convergence with transnational organised crime* (2015), pp. 1–20. http://www.tandfonline.com.ezproxy-f.deakin.edu.au/doi/full/10.1080/09546553.2015.1089863. Accessed 14 August 2017.

E.D. Mainas, The analysis of criminal and terrorist organisations as social network structures: a quasi-experimental study. *Int. J. Police Sci. Manag.* **14**(3), 264–283 (2012)

A. Malm, G. Bichler, Networks of collaborating criminals: assessing the structural vulnerability of drug markets. *J. Res. Crime Delinq.* **48**(2), 271–297 (2011)

A.J. Masys (ed.), *Networks and network analysis for defence and security* (Springer, Switzerland, 2014)

C. McGrath, J. Blythe, D. Krackhardt, The effect of spatial arrangement on judgments and errors in interpreting graphs. *Soc. Networks* **19**(3), 223–242 (1997)

C. McGrath, D. Krackhardt, J. Blythe, Visualizing complexity in networks: seeing both the forest and the trees. *Connect* **25**(1), 37–47 (2003)

R.M. Medina, Social network analysis: a case study of the Islamist terrorist network. *Secur. J.* **27**(1), 97–121 (2014)

J.F. Morris, R.F. Deckro, SNA data difficulties with dark networks. *Behav. Sci. Terrorism Polit. Aggression* **5**(2), 70–93 (2013)

C. Morselli, Assessing vulnerable and strategic positions in a criminal network. *J. Contemp. Crim. Justice* **26**(4), 382–392 (2010)

C. Morselli (ed.), *Crime and networks* (Routledge, New York, 2014)

S. Mullins, Social network analysis and counter-terrorism: measures of centrality as an investigative tool. *Behav. Sci. Terrorism Polit. Aggression* **5**(2), 115–136 (2012)

R. Nash, M. Bouchard, A. Malm, Investing in people: the role of social networks in the diffusion of a large-scale fraud. *Soc. Networks* **35**(4), 686–698 (2013)

M. Natarajan, Understanding the structure of a large heroin distribution network: a quantitative analysis of qualitative data. *J. Quant. Criminol.* **22**(2), 171–192 (2006)

NCPE, *Guidance on the National Intelligence Model*, Intelligence Solutions (2005). https://www.intelligencesolutions.co.nz/media/1715/guidance%20on%20the%20nim%202005.pdf. Accessed 10 January 2017.

A.V. Papachristos, Murder by structure: dominance relations and the social structure of gang homicide. *Am. J. Sociol.* **115**(1), 74–128 (2009)

A. Perliger, A. Pedahzur, Social network analysis in the study of terrorism and political violence. *Polit. Sci. Polit.* **44**(2), 45–50 (2011)

S.W. Phillips, The attitudes of police managers toward intelligence-led policing. *FBI Law Enforce. Bull.* **81**(9), 13–17 (2012)

J. Ratcliffe, The effectiveness of police intelligence management: A New Zealand case study. *Police Pract. Res.* **6**(5), 435–451 (2005)

J. Ratcliffe, *Intelligence-led policing* (Routledge, New York, 2016)

D.K. Rossmo, *Criminal investigative failures* (CRC Press, New York, 2009)

C.B. Sanders, S. Henderson, Police 'empires' and information technologies: uncovering material and organisational barriers to information sharing in Canadian police services. *Polic. Soc.* **23**(2), 243–260 (2013)

C.B. Sanders, C. Weston, N. Schott, Police innovations, 'secret squirrels' and accountability: Empirically studying intelligence-led policing in Canada. *Br. J. Criminol.* **55**(4), 711–729 (2015)

D.M. Schwartz, T. Rouselle, Using social network analysis to target criminal networks. *Trends Org. Crime* **12**(2), 188–207 (2009)

J. Scott, P. J. Carrington (eds.), *The SAGE handbook of social network analysis* (SAGE Publications, London, 2011)

J. Sheptycki, Organizational pathologies in police intelligence systems: some contributions to the lexicon of intelligence-led policing. *Eur. J. Criminol.* **1**(3), 307–332 (2004)

J. Sheptycki, The police intelligence division-of-labour. Polic. Soc. **27**(6), 620–635 (2017)

M.K. Sparrow, The application of network analysis to criminal intelligence: an assessment of the prospects. *Soc. Networks* **13**(3), 251–274 (1991)

I.P. Stainer, *Contemporary organisational pathologies in police information sharing: new contributions to Sheptycki's lexicon of intelligence-led policing*, Doctor of Philosophy thesis, London Metropolitan University, 2013.

E. Stollenwerk, T. Dörfler, J. Schibberges, Taking a new perspective: mapping the Al Qaeda network through the eyes of the UN Security Council. *Terror. Political Violence* **28**(5), 950–970 (2016)

S.J. Strang, Network analysis in criminal intelligence, in *Networks and network analysis for defence and security*, ed. by A. J. Masys, (Springer International Publishing, Cham, 2014), pp. 1–26

B. Taylor, A. Kowalyk, R. Boba, The integration of crime analysis into law enforcement agencies: an exploratory study into the perceptions of crime analysts. *Police Q.* **10**(154), 154–169 (2007)

R.W. Taylor, E.J. Fritsch, J. Liederbach, *Digital crime and digital terrorism* (Prentice Hall Press, New Jersey, 2014)

R. van der Hulst, Introduction to social network analysis (SNA) as an investigative tool. *Trends Org. Crime* **12**(2), 101–121 (2009)

F. Varese, The structure and the content of criminal connections: the Russian mafia in Italy. *European Sociological Review* **29**(5), 899–909 (2013)

C. Whelan, *Networks and national security: dynamics, effectiveness and organisation* (Ashgate, London, 2012)

J. Xu, H. Chen, Criminal network analysis and visualization. *Commun. ACM* **48**(6), 100–107 (2005)

J. Xu, H. Chen, The topology of dark networks. *Commun. ACM* **51**(10), 58–65 (2008)

J. Xu, B. Marshall, S. Kaza, H. Chen, Analyzing and visualizing criminal network dynamics: a case study, in *Intelligence and Security Informatics*, ed. by H. Chen, R. Moore, D. D. Zeng, J. Leavitt, vol. 3073, (Springer, Berlin/Heidelberg, 2004), pp. 359–377

Index[1]

---

[1] Note: Page numbers followed by 'n' refer to notes.